"This series is a tremendous resource for   le with an understanding of how the gospel is wov   :l-minded pastors and scholars doing gospel busines   and theo- logical feast preparing God's people to ap   and mind wholly committed to Christ's priorities."

     BRYAN CHAPELL, President Emeritus, Covenant Theological Seminary; Senior Pastor, Grace Presbyterian Church, Peoria, Illinois

"Mark Twain may have smiled when he wrote to a friend, 'I didn't have time to write you a short letter, so I wrote you a long letter.' But the truth of Twain's remark remains serious and universal, because well-reasoned, compact writing requires extra time and extra hard work. And this is what we have in the Crossway Bible study series *Knowing the Bible*. The skilled authors and notable editors provide the contours of each book of the Bible as well as the grand theological themes that bind them together as one Book. Here, in a 12-week format, are carefully wrought studies that will ignite the mind and the heart."

     R. KENT HUGHES, Visiting Professor of Practical Theology, Westminster Theological Seminary

"*Knowing the Bible* brings together a gifted team of Bible teachers to produce a high-quality series of study guides. The coordinated focus of these materials is unique: biblical content, provocative questions, systematic theology, practical application, and the gospel story of God's grace presented all the way through Scripture."

     PHILIP G. RYKEN, President, Wheaton College

"These *Knowing the Bible* volumes provide a significant and very welcome variation on the general run of inductive Bible studies. This series provides substantial instruction, as well as teaching through the very questions that are asked. *Knowing the Bible* then goes even further by showing how any given text links with the gospel, the whole Bible, and the formation of theology. I heartily endorse this orientation of individual books to the whole Bible and the gospel, and I applaud the demonstration that sound theology was not something invented later by Christians, but is right there in the pages of Scripture."

     GRAEME L. GOLDSWORTHY, former lecturer, Moore Theological College; author, *According to Plan, Gospel and Kingdom, The Gospel in Revelation*, and *Gospel and Wisdom*

"What a gift to earnest, Bible-loving, Bible-searching believers! The organization and structure of the Bible study format presented through the *Knowing the Bible* series is so well conceived. Students of the Word are led to understand the content of passages through per-ceptive, guided questions, and they are given rich insights and application all along the way in the brief but illuminating sections that conclude each study. What potential growth in depth and breadth of understanding these studies offer! One can only pray that vast numbers of believers will discover more of God and the beauty of his Word through these rich studies."

     BRUCE A. WARE, Professor of Christian Theology, The Southern Baptist Theological Seminary

KNOWING THE BIBLE

J. I. Packer, Theological Editor
Dane C. Ortlund, Series Editor
Lane T. Dennis, Executive Editor

•   •   •   •   •   •

Genesis	Psalms	Jonah, Micah, and Nahum	Ephesians
Exodus	Proverbs		Philippians
Leviticus	Ecclesiastes	Haggai, Zechariah, and Malachi	Colossians and Philemon
Numbers	Song of Solomon		
Deuteronomy	Isaiah	Matthew	1–2 Thessalonians
Joshua	Jeremiah	Mark	1–2 Timothy and Titus
Judges	Lamentations, Habakkuk, and Zephaniah	Luke	
Ruth and Esther		John	Hebrews
1–2 Samuel	Ezekiel	Acts	James
1–2 Kings	Daniel	Romans	1–2 Peter and Jude
1–2 Chronicles	Hosea	1 Corinthians	1–3 John
Ezra and Nehemiah	Joel, Amos, and Obadiah	2 Corinthians	Revelation
Job		Galatians	

•   •   •   •   •   •

J. I. PACKER was the former Board of Governors' Professor of Theology at Regent College (Vancouver, BC). Dr. Packer earned his DPhil at the University of Oxford. He is known and loved worldwide as the author of the best-selling book *Knowing God*, as well as many other titles on theology and the Christian life. He served as the General Editor of the ESV Bible and as the Theological Editor for the *ESV Study Bible*.

LANE T. DENNIS is CEO of Crossway, a not-for-profit publishing ministry. Dr. Dennis earned his PhD from Northwestern University. He is Chair of the ESV Bible Translation Oversight Committee and Executive Editor of the *ESV Study Bible*.

DANE C. ORTLUND (PhD, Wheaton College) serves as senior pastor of Naperville Presbyterian Church in Naperville, Illinois. He is an editor for the Knowing the Bible series and the Short Studies in Biblical Theology series, and is the author of several books, including *Gentle and Lowly: The Heart of Christ for Sinners and Sufferers*.

GENESIS

A 12-WEEK STUDY

Mitchell M. Kim

WHEATON, ILLINOIS

Knowing the Bible: Genesis, A 12-Week Study

Copyright © 2013 by Crossway

Published by Crossway
        1300 Crescent Street
        Wheaton, Illinois 60187

Some content used in this study guide has been adapted from the *ESV Study Bible*, copyright © 2008 by Crossway, pages 49–137. Used by permission. All rights reserved.

Cover design: Simplicated Studio

First printing 2013

Printed in the United States of America

Trade paperback ISBN: 978-1-4335-3501-7
PDF ISBN: 978-1-4335-3502-4
Mobipocket ISBN: 978-1-4335-3503-1
EPub ISBN: 978-1-4335-3504-8

Crossway is a publishing ministry of Good News Publishers.

VP		30	29	28	27	26	25	24	23	22
20	19	18	17	16	15	14	13	12	11	10

TABLE OF CONTENTS

SERIES PREFACE

KNOWING THE BIBLE, as the series title indicates, was created to help readers know and understand the meaning, the message, and the God of the Bible. Each volume in the series consists of 12 units that progressively take the reader through a clear, concise study of that book of the Bible. In this way, any given volume can fruitfully be used in a 12-week format either in group study, such as in a church-based context, or in individual study. Of course, these 12 studies could be completed in fewer or more than 12 weeks, as convenient, depending on the context in which they are used.

Each study unit gives an overview of the text at hand before digging into it with a series of questions for reflection or discussion. The unit then concludes by highlighting the gospel of grace in each passage ("Gospel Glimpses"), identifying whole-Bible themes that occur in the passage ("Whole-Bible Connections"), and pinpointing Christian doctrines that are affirmed in the passage ("Theological Soundings").

The final component to each unit is a section for reflecting on personal and practical implications from the passage at hand. The layout provides space for recording responses to the questions proposed, and we think readers need to do this to get the full benefit of the exercise. The series also includes definitions of key words. These definitions are indicated by a note number in the text and are found at the end of each chapter.

Lastly, to help understand the Bible in this deeper way, we urge readers to use the ESV Bible and the *ESV Study Bible*, which are available in various print and digital formats, including online editions at esv.org. The Knowing the Bible series is also available online.

May the Lord greatly bless your study as you seek to know him through knowing his Word.

J. I. Packer
Lane T. Dennis

Week 1: Overview

Getting Acquainted

In Genesis, God's purposes for the heavens and earth, distorted by sin spreading through all the earth, are focused in one man: Abraham. Through him and his family God would bring blessing to all nations.

Despite God's good purposes for creation, sin enters and fills the earth (the primeval history[1]; chs. 1–11), and so God moves his plan forward to bless the nations through the offspring of Abraham (the patriarchal history[2]; chs. 12–50). Genesis is foundational to the whole Bible, and to every human life. Genesis tells us who God is, who we are, how things went wrong, and the plan that God has put in place to return the earth to the way it was meant to be.

Placing It in the Larger Story

Many readers miss the forest of God's larger purposes when immersed in the trees of each individual story. In creation, God creates humanity in his own image as his representatives to fill and rule the earth on his behalf (Gen. 1:26–28). Even after Adam and Eve sin and are punished, the promise is given that the offspring of the woman will defeat the serpent and restore the earth (Gen. 3:15). This promise is traced throughout the book in its genealogies,[3] which provide the backbone of the entire book. Key divisions are traced by "These are the generations of," tracing out the stories of key figures, starting with "the heavens and the earth" (2:4–4:26), and going on to Adam (5:1–6:8),

Noah (6:9–9:29), the sons of Noah (10:1–11:19), Shem (11:10–26), Terah (11:27–25:11), Ishmael (25:12–18), Isaac (25:19–35:29), Esau (36:1–37:1), and Jacob (37:2–50:26). The line of God's blessing is emphasized (e.g., Adam, Noah, Terah, Isaac, Jacob), while the stories of other lines receive less attention (e.g., Ishmael, Esau). The individual stories of Abraham, Jacob and Joseph are illustrations of how the promise of Genesis 3:15 begins to be fulfilled.

God desires to bless the nations through a future king. Adam is portrayed in the image of God, a phrase probably signifying a royal representative of God. Abraham would become a "great nation" (Gen. 12:2), and "kings shall come from you" (Gen. 17:6). God's original command to "Be fruitful and multiply and fill the earth" (Gen. 1:28) is fulfilled in microcosm[4] as "Israel settled in the land of Egypt . . . and were fruitful and multiplied greatly" (Gen. 47:27; cf. 1:28).

Israel fails, however, in its calling to be a "kingdom of priests" (Ex. 19:6). This priesthood is ultimately fulfilled through the church in Jesus Christ as a "royal priesthood" of all nations (1 Pet. 2:9). Through this priesthood, God's purposes for creation as detailed in Genesis 1–2 are finally accomplished, as is seen in Revelation 21–22.

Key Verse

"And God blessed them. And God said to them, 'Be fruitful and multiply and fill the earth and subdue it, and have dominion over the fish of the sea and over the birds of the heavens and over every living thing that moves on the earth." (Gen. 1:28)

Date and Historical Background

With the other books of the Pentateuch (Exodus, Leviticus, Numbers, and Deuteronomy), Genesis has been ascribed to Moses. Although Mosaic authorship has been questioned by some, numerous parallels with other ancient Near Eastern literature in the second millennium BC confirm the plausibility of the traditional view.

Outline

I. Primeval History (1:1–11:26)

  A. God's creation and the ordering of heaven and earth (1:1–2:3)

  B. Humanity and sin in the world (2:4–3:24)

  C. The downward spiral of sin in the world (4:1–11:26)

II. Patriarchal History (11:27–50:26)

    A. Abraham and the covenant (11:27–16:16)

    B. Abraham and obedience (17:1–22:24)

    C. From Abraham to Isaac (23:1–26:33)

    D. Jacob: consequences of deception (26:34—31:55)

    E. Jacob: reconciliation with Esau (32:1–35:29)

    F. Joseph: dreams and affliction (36:1–41:57)

    G. Joseph: reconciliation with brothers (42:1–47:31)

    H. Blessing of Jacob (48:1–50:26)

As You Get Started

Besides the individual stories in Genesis, how do you see the themes and trajectories laid out in this book developed in the rest of the Bible? In your view, how does Genesis play a foundational role for the entire Bible?

The entire book of Genesis is framed by genealogies. What important role might be played by these otherwise boring lists of names in tracing out the many promises that we find in this book?

What perplexes you about this book? What questions do you hope to see answered by this study of Genesis?

> ## As You Finish This Unit . . .

Come before God with humility in prayer and ask for the Spirit who inspired Scripture to illuminate your mind to understand Genesis in all its riches. Ask him to strengthen and deepen your understanding of God's foundational purposes for creation and the glory of his purposes in redemption. Pray that God might soften your heart to hear the still small voice of God's Spirit. Take some time to go back over this study and reflect on what the Lord might be teaching you, especially noting areas and questions that you would like to explore further through this study.

Definitions

[1] **Primeval history** – The earliest history of the Bible from the creation of the world (Genesis 1) to the Tower of Babel (Genesis 11).

[2] **Patriarchal history** – A history of the patriarchs (fathers) of the Old Testament, primarily Abraham, Isaac, and Jacob.

[3] **Genealogy** – The study of the lineage of families; genealogies are particularly important in Genesis as it traces the preservation of the offspring of the woman who will ultimately defeat the offspring of the serpent.

[4] **Macrocosm/microcosm** – Macrocosm is the big picture, while microcosm is a more specific picture that nevertheless represents the big picture. The macrocosm of Genesis 1–11 focuses on the whole earth, while the microcosm of Genesis 12–50 focuses on one family, the line of Abraham.

Week 2: Creation

Genesis 1:1–2:3

"Where do we come from?" Children's questions can be both simple and profound, and our answer to this question affects the way we view the entire world. The answer is given in this opening section of Genesis. The primeval history of Genesis 1–11 provides a wide-lens, macrocosmic picture of God's purposes for the world. This is followed by the narrow-lens, microcosmic drama in Genesis 12–50 of God's promises passed down through the generations of Abraham, Isaac, and Jacob. Martin Luther reminds us that these opening chapters are "certainly the foundation of the whole of Scripture." Genesis 1 begins "In the beginning, God," reminding us that it all starts with God, and thus Genesis sets the stage for everything that follows.

The Big Picture

God creates the heavens and the earth and places humanity at earth's pinnacle with a commission to populate the earth as his image-bearers.

> ### Reflection and Discussion

Read through the entire text for this study, Genesis 1:1–2:3. Then interact with the following questions and record your notes on them concerning this section of Genesis. (For further background, see the *ESV Study Bible*, pages 49–53; also available online at esv.org.)

Repeated words or phrases indicate their importance. What words and phrases are repeated throughout Genesis 1:1–2:3? Take time to reflect on each of these repeated phrases and their significance.

Although "the earth was without form and void" (Gen. 1:2), God forms the earth (days 1–3) and then fills it (days 4–6). Place the days of creation on the following chart.

Day	What was created? (God Forms)	Day	What was created? (God Fills)
1		4	
2		5	
3		6	
7 God rests			

One repeated phrase is, "And there was evening, and there was morning, the _____ day" (Gen. 1:5, 8, 13, 19, 23, 31). What does this rhythm and balance of God's orderly creation communicate?

Another repeated phrase is "And God said" (Gen. 1:3, 6, 9, 11, 14, 20, 24, 26, 29). This word which God speaks creates. The creative power of God's word is stressed throughout Scripture (e.g., Isa. 55:10–11; John 1:3; Rom 4:17). How does the creative power of God's word strengthen our resolve to meditate on the written Word of God in our own lives?

Another refrain throughout this passage is that, "God saw that it was good" (Gen. 1:10, 12, 18, 21, 25), culminating in God seeing "everything that he had made, and behold, it was very good" (Gen. 1:31). Some idolize creation as God, while others despise creation as evil. But these are two equally wrong extremes. What suggestions for a proper relationship between humanity and creation are provided in Genesis 1?

Chapter 1 climaxes with the creation of humanity (Gen. 1:26–31). Note the ways in which this final creative act of God is different from the previous creative acts of God. How is the distinctiveness of humanity emphasized in 1:26–31?

What is the distinctive purpose for humanity in God's creation?

The climax of the week of creation is God's Sabbath rest on the seventh day (Gen. 2:3). Similarly, the seventh speech for the building of the tabernacle climaxes with instructions on the Sabbath (Ex. 31:12–17). God's Sabbath rest hints at the purpose of creation, since divine rest is associated with temple building in other ancient Near Eastern accounts, as well as elsewhere in the Old Testament. Similarly, just as "And God said" frames his seven days of creation, so "And Yahweh said" frames the seven speeches for the creation of the tabernacle[1] (Ex. 25:1; 30:11, 17, 22, 34; 31:1, 12). The psalmist explicitly compares the building of the sanctuary[2] to the creation of the heavens and earth (Ps. 78:69). In light of all this, how should an understanding of the heavens and earth as a divine sanctuary affect our understanding of the purpose of the cosmos?

Read through the following three sections on *Gospel Glimpses*, *Whole-Bible Connections*, and *Theological Soundings*. Then take time to reflect on the *Personal Implications* these sections may have for your walk with the Lord.

Gospel Glimpses

THE POWER OF GOD'S WORD. We clearly and unequivocally see the power of God's Word in this passage. God creates by the power of his Word (cf. John

1:1–3). This same Word "became flesh and dwelt among us, and we have seen his glory, glory as of the only Son from the Father, full of grace and truth" (John 1:14). The Word active in creation is revealed as a Person who becomes flesh and blood in redemption[3] to come and save.

REST. When God finished his work, "he rested on the seventh day from all his work that he had done" (Gen. 2:2). He did not rest because he was tired, but to enjoy the world that he had worked to create. In Christ, this rest is fulfilled, so that "there remains a Sabbath rest for the people of God" (Heb. 4:9). Jesus offers the key to enter that rest, since he invites us, "Come to me, all who labor and are heavy laden, and I will give you rest" (Matt. 11:28). In creation, the pattern was work then rest. In the gospel, the pattern is rest then work (1 Cor. 15:9–10; Phil. 2:12–13).

Whole-Bible Connections

IMAGE OF GOD. Humanity is created in the image of God, and this image is expressed in the use of God-given rational and relational power and also in ruling and subduing the creation. This image of God is passed down the generations through the line of Seth (Genesis 5). However, this image was distorted by the fall and is not seen in fully reconstituted form until the coming of Jesus Christ, the ultimate "image of God" (2 Cor. 4:4; Col. 1:15). Those who believe in Christ are being recreated and transformed into that image (2 Cor. 3:18), and this process of transformation will be made complete when we rise again (1 Cor. 15:49). Presently, we know that "all things work together for good, for those who are called according to his purpose," a purpose which is "to be conformed to the image of his Son" (Rom. 8:28–29).

SUBDUING THE BEASTS. While Adam was to subdue the beasts, he was himself subdued by a beast, the serpent. The failure of the first Adam looks forward to the coming of a Second Adam, the Son of Man, who would, like Adam, subdue the beasts of the earth (Ps. 8:4–8; Dan. 7:13–14). Jesus is this Son of Man (Matt. 9:6; 25:31; 28:18), who subdued the wild beasts after his temptation in the wilderness (Mark 1:13). By the authority of this Son of Man over all heaven and earth, we are to make all nations disciples to him (Matt. 28:18–20). We should not be subject to the deception of the serpent like the first Adam but move forward with confidence since "the God of peace will soon crush Satan[4] under [our] feet" (Rom. 16:20).

BE FRUITFUL, MULTIPLY, AND FILL THE EARTH. God called Adam to "be fruitful and multiply and fill the earth" (Gen. 1:28) with his descendants as images and representatives of God. This call is passed down to Noah (Gen. 9:1, 7), Abraham (12:2–3; 22:17), Isaac (26:4), and Jacob (28:3–4). While it begins to be fulfilled in a small way in Egypt (Ex. 1:7), this call looks forward after the exile to a more global fulfillment (Jer. 23:3). This call is transformed by the coming of Jesus Christ with a focus on spiritual progeny birthed by the power of the word of God. As a result, the word of God increases ("increase" = "to bear fruit"; the same Greek word is used in Gen. 1:28 in the Greek Old Testament translation used by the apostles) and multiplies in Jerusalem (Acts 6:7), Judea and Samaria (12:24) and to the end of the earth (19:20). These are the key markers of the gospel's progress in the book of Acts (1:8). In Colossians, similarly, Paul celebrates how "the word of truth, the gospel . . . has come to you, as indeed in the whole world [and] is *bearing fruit* and *increasing*" (Col. 1:5–6), so that they might walk, "*bearing fruit* in every good work and *increasing* in the knowledge of God" (v. 10). Through Christ, Christians fill the earth as images and representatives of God by the power of the gospel.

Theological Soundings

TRINITY. God the Father is the Creator (Gen. 1:1) who works with the Spirit (v. 2) by the power of his Word (v. 3) to create the heavens and the earth. All three persons of the Trinity are at work in this opening chapter of Scripture. A glimpse of the Trinity can perhaps also be seen in the plural of Genesis 1:26: "Let *us* make man in our image, after our likeness." While some see this plural referring to God speaking to his heavenly court of angels (as in, e.g., Job 1:6), humanity is not made in the image of angels, and we have no indication that angels participated in the creation of human beings. This glimpse of the Trinity is filled out with more detail through the progressive revelation of Scripture.

CREATION. God surveys his creation and calls it "good" (Gen. 1:4, 10, 12, 18, 21, 25) and "very good" (v. 31). God's good creation calls for humanity's wise stewardship (vv. 26–28). We can worship God not only by looking at his Word but also by appreciating his works demonstrated throughout all creation. "The heavens declare the glory of God, and the sky above proclaims his handiwork" (Ps. 19:1).

HUMANITY. The climax of this chapter is found in the creation of humanity. The largest number of verses is devoted to this day of creation. Only humanity is created by God in community (Gen. 1:26), in the image of God (vv. 26–27), and is given dominion over the animals (v. 28) and the fruits of the earth for food (v. 29). No wonder the psalmist celebrates, "you have made him [humanity, a collective noun] a little lower than the heavenly beings and crowned him with glory and honor. You have given him dominion over the works of your hands; you have put all things under his feet, all sheep and oxen, and also the beasts of the field, the birds of the heavens, and the fish of the sea, whatever passes along the paths of the seas" (Ps. 8:5–8).

▶ **Personal Implications**

Take some time to reflect on the personal implications of Genesis 1:1–2:3 for your life today. Jot down your reflections under the three headings we have considered and on the passage as a whole:

1. Gospel Glimpses

2. Whole-Bible Connections

3. Theological Soundings

4. Genesis 1:1–2:3

As You Finish This Unit . . .

Pray that God would seal the insights that you have obtained about God's purposes in creation. May the riches of this chapter move your heart to marvel at the greatness of God in greater measure. Highlight a few areas for further reflection to come back to at a later time.

Definitions

[1] **Tabernacle** – The tent where God dwelled on earth and communed with his people as Israel's divine king. The temple in Jerusalem later replaced it.

[2] **Sanctuary** – A place set aside as holy because of God's presence there. The inner sanctuary of the tabernacle and the temple was called the Most Holy Place.

[3] **Redemption** – The act of buying back someone who had become enslaved or something that had been lost to someone else. Through his death and resurrection, Jesus purchased redemption for all believers (Col. 1:13–14).

[4] **Satan** – A spiritual being whose name means "accuser." As the leader of all the demonic forces, he opposes God's rule and seeks to harm God's people and accuse them of wrongdoing. One day he will be destroyed along with all his demons (Matt. 25:41; Rev. 20:10).

WEEK 3: HUMANITY'S PURPOSE AND FAILURE

Genesis 2:4–3:24

The Place of the Passage

Genesis 2:4–25 amplifies in greater detail the compressed statement of God's purpose for humanity in 1:26–31. The terse, poetic language of chapter 1 is explained in a narrative of the creation of humanity in the garden-sanctuary of Eden in chapter 2. When God's command to Adam and Eve in 2:16–17 is disobeyed in chapter 3, at the instigation of the serpent, consequences ensue for everyone involved. Sin[1] invades the universe. Nevertheless, God's grace[2] still abounds in his judgment,[3] as the offspring of the woman will conquer the serpent (3:15) and procreation and dominion will continue, though only through pain (vv. 16–19).

The Big Picture

Humanity, the crown and pinnacle of creation with a commission to fill the earth with image-bearers, fails in that calling and faces consequences.

▶ **Reflection and Discussion**

Read through the entire text for this study, Genesis 2:4–3:24. Then interact with the following questions and record your notes on them concerning this section of Genesis. (For further background, see the *ESV Study Bible*, pages 53–57; also available online at esv.org.)

God's Purpose for Humanity (Genesis 2)

God's special role for humanity seen in Genesis 1:26–30 is amplified in chapter 2. How is God's special blessing on humanity evident (2:4–9)?

Many scholars recognize Eden as the first sanctuary and dwelling place of God, corresponding to the later temple. Just as a river "flowed out of Eden to water the garden" next to the tree of life (Gen. 2:10–14), so in the Bible's climactic vision a river flows from the presence of God in the temple, surrounded by trees that bring life (Ezek. 47:1–12; Rev. 22:1–2). Also, this river is surrounded by gold, bdellium, and onyx stone (Gen. 2:12), just as gold filled the temple (e.g., Rev 21:18), bdellium recalled the manna (Num. 11:7) in the ark of the covenant, and onyx stones were placed on the clothing of the priests (Ex. 25:7; 28:9). Finally, after sin enters the garden, cherubim[4] protect the garden and tree of life from unclean humanity (Gen. 3:24), just as the cherubim guard the ark of the covenant (Ex. 37:7–9; 1 Sam. 4:4). Indeed, "he built his sanctuary like the high heavens, like the earth, which he has founded forever" (Ps. 78:69), and Eden is called "the garden of God" and "the holy mountain of God" (Ezek. 28:13, 14). Consider the significance of Eden as the first temple. If Eden is the sanctuary of God, what does that tell us about the whole cosmos, or about Adam's role?

Just as Adam was to "to *work* and *keep*" the garden sanctuary of Eden (Gen. 2:15), so the priests were to *keep* "all the furnishings of the tent of meeting . . . as they minister at the tabernacle" (Num. 3:8). What does this teach us about Adam's role? Consider also that Jesus, the Second Adam (1 Cor. 15:45), was himself the final priest (Heb. 7:23–28).

In Genesis 2:18–25, how does God provide help for Adam to fulfill his calling?

Humanity's Failure (Genesis 3)

While Adam and Eve were to care for the sanctuary of Eden by subduing the beasts and obeying God's word (Gen. 1:28; 2:15–17), they end up being subdued by a beast by compromising God's word and are exiled from the sanctuary of Eden (3:24). Compare carefully how God's instructions are subtly changed from God's original instructions in 2:16–17 to their recollection in 3:1–5. What changes do you see?

In what ways do these subtle changes to God's word reflect a distorted picture of God's character in Genesis 3:1–5?

21

Look carefully at the consequences of sin in Genesis 3:7–13. How does sin break down relationships, both vertically between God and humanity, and horizontally between Adam and Eve?

For this sin, God's punishment is swift and sure. Describe the punishment for each of the following, noting how Adam and Eve's punishments link up with their original calling in Genesis 1:28:

Serpent:

Adam:

Eve:

However, even in the midst of punishment, God's grace and gospel are evident. Describe the promise that is present even in the punishment of Adam and Eve:

Adam:

Eve:

_____

_____

_____

_____

How is God's grace evident in Genesis 3:20–21? What hints do we have about the coming sacrificial system and Jesus, the "Lamb of God, who takes away the sin of the world" (John 1:29)?

_____

_____

_____

_____

_____

Read through the following three sections on *Gospel Glimpses, Whole-Bible Connections,* and *Theological Soundings.* Then take time to reflect on the *Personal Implications* these sections may have for your walk with the Lord.

▶ Gospel Glimpses

PROTO-EUANGELIUM. Genesis 3:15 is widely seen to be the proto-euangelium ("early gospel"), the earliest declaration of the divine grace of the gospel. Although the serpent would bruise the heel of the offspring of the woman, the offspring of the woman would crush the head of the serpent. As a result, Genesis focuses on the offspring of the woman by tracing this line through many genealogies. The hopes of this offspring and seed of the woman finally crystallize around the seed of David. Eventually, the serpent does bruise the heel of Jesus at the cross, but Jesus crushes his head at the resurrection. Furthermore, a glorious promise is given to those who are in Christ, that "the God of peace will soon crush Satan under your feet" (Rom. 16:20).

GOD'S GRACE EVEN IN PUNISHMENT. Although Genesis 3 ends with the account of God's punishment for Adam and Eve, his promise endures even in the face of his punishment. Though Eve will have pain in childbearing, she will still bring forth children. Though Adam will have pain in eating what comes from the ground, the ground will still produce food for him. Disobedience does not remove them completely from the realm of God's promise, but this promise endures even in the face of their disobedience.

GARMENTS OF SKIN. The first animal is killed to clothe Adam and Eve's nakedness in Genesis 3:21. Though nakedness did not cause them shame before the fall, sin immediately brought shame at their nakedness, so that they hide themselves (Gen. 3:8). However, God covers their nakedness with the skin of an animal. This looks forward to the ministry of the Lamb of God, who takes away the sin of the world (John 1:29; cf. Zech. 3:1–5). In a similar manner, we are to "cast off the works of darkness and put on the armor of light," which is to "put on the Lord Jesus Christ" (Rom. 13:12, 14; cf. Eph. 4:22–24; Col. 3:9–10).

Whole-Bible Connections

THE RIVER FROM EDEN. The careful reader will notice that the river flows "out of Eden to water the garden" (Gen. 2:10), outside of which are the nations such as Cush (2:11–14). Just as there was a gradation of holiness in the temple from God's presence (the holy of holies) to where the priests ministered (the holy place), and from there to the outer court of the Gentiles, so there is a gradation of holiness from God's presence (Eden) to the place where the first priest Adam ministered (the garden), and from there to the nations outside the garden. Similarly, just as the river flows from God's presence in Eden through the garden to the nations, so the water of the temple flows from God's presence through the holy place to the nations (Ezek. 47:1–12) to bring healing to the nations (Rev. 22:2). In the new earth, a river will flow once more (Rev. 22:1), this time with no need for a temple—since the restored fellowship anticipated by the temple is finally achieved by the work of Christ (Rev. 21:22).

FIRST ADAM, SECOND ADAM. Where Adam failed in his confrontation with the serpent in Genesis 3, the second Adam Jesus succeeds. When Jesus, the "son of Adam" (Luke 3:38) confronted the serpent (4:3), he did not take what was "good for food" (Gen. 3:6) but declared "man shall not live by bread alone" (Luke 4:4), refused what was "a delight to the eyes" (Gen. 3:6) when he saw "all the kingdoms of the world" (Luke 4:5–6), and was not led astray by what would "make one wise" (Gen. 3:6) by casting himself down from the pinnacle of the temple (Luke 4:9–12). As a result, "as one trespass [of the first Adam] led to condemnation for all men, so one act of righteousness [by the second Adam] leads to justification and life for all men" (Rom 5:18).

Theological Soundings

WORD OF GOD. The weeds of sin grow quickly when God's Word has not taken root in our hearts. As John Calvin reminds us:

> And surely, once we hold God's Word in contempt, we shake off all reverence for him! . . . . For Adam would never have dared oppose God's

authority unless he had disbelieved in God's Word. Here, indeed, was the best bridle to control all passions: the thought that nothing is better than to practice righteousness by obeying God's commandments; then, that the ultimate goal of the happy life is to be loved by him. Therefore Adam, carried away by the devil's blasphemies, as far as he was able extinguished the whole glory of God. (*Institutes of the Christian Religion*, 2.1.4)

The serpent did not tempt with radical departures from God's command in Genesis 3 or Luke 4 but only slight deviations. However, the best "bridle to control all passions" is the power of God's word. This illustrates the truth of the psalmist: "I have stored up your word in my heart, that I might not sin against you" (Ps. 119:11).

THEOLOGY AND OBEDIENCE. Our view of God directly affects our view of obedience. Instead of referring to God as the covenant keeping LORD (*Yahweh*) God, Eve simply refers to him as the distant God (*Elohim*) of power who created all things (Gen. 3:3). While God lavishly allows them to "eat of every tree of the garden" (2:16), Eve minimizes God's permission by saying, "We may eat of the fruit of the trees in the garden" (3:2). Although God commands them not to eat of the forbidden tree, Eve maximizes the prohibition by adding "neither shall you touch it" (3:3). While God warns "you shall surely die" (2:17), Eve minimizes the consequences of sin by saying only "lest you die" (3:3). These subtle changes neglect the lavish character of God in covenant relationship to his people and instead reflect a concept of God as a stingy kill-joy who robs his people of life. With such a twisted view of God, no wonder Eve disobeys!

WORK. Work is not a result of the fall. Meaningful work was present even before the fall (Gen. 2:15). Although the fall brought pain and toil to our work (3:17–19), work itself is part of God's perfect plan in the sanctuary of creation.

DEATH. God warned that if they would eat of the tree of the knowledge of good and evil, they would "surely die" (Gen. 2:17). The serpent said, "You will not surely die" (3:4), and it is true that they did not die physically. However, they were immediately exiled in general from the abundant and verdant life in Eden (2:8–14) and in particular from the tree of life (3:24). Furthermore, a sentence of death is pronounced on the day of Adam's sin that is executed later (see similarly the sentence of death on Shimei in 1 Kings 2:37–46). In this way, "the wages of sin is death" (Rom. 6:23).

> ## Personal Implications

Take some time to reflect on the personal implications of Genesis 2:4–3:24 for your life today. Jot down your reflections under the three headings we have considered and on the passage as a whole:

1. Gospel Glimpses

2. Whole-Bible Connections

3. Theological Soundings

4. Genesis 2:4–3:24

As You Finish This Unit . . .

Pray that God would seal the insights that you have obtained about his purposes for humanity and the consequences of sin. May the riches of this chapter move your heart to marvel at the grace of God even in judgment. Highlight a few areas for further reflection to come back to at a later time.

Definitions

[1] **Sin** – Any violation of or failure to adhere to the commands of God, or the desire to do so.

[2] **Grace** – Unmerited favor, especially the free gift of salvation that God gives to believers through faith in Jesus Christ.

[3] **Judgment** – Any assessment of something or someone, especially moral assessment. The Bible also speaks of a final day of judgment when Christ returns, when all those who have refused to repent will be judged and punished (Rev. 20:12–15).

[4] **Cherubim** – Angelic guardians of the holy places.

Week 4: The Downward Spiral of Sin

Genesis 4:1–11:26

> ## The Place of the Passage

Sometimes sin has immediate consequences; sometimes it does not. In the previous chapter, we saw sin's immediate consequences. Adam and Eve realized they were naked, they hid from God, and God punished them for their sins. In the next major section in Genesis, we see the longer-term consequences of sin—how it just seems to get worse and worse. The scope of Genesis 4–11 is macrocosmic (big picture): instead of the earth being filled with representatives of God, the earth is filled with the consequences of sin. Nevertheless, God's grace abounds even in the face of our sin. Glimpses of his mercy are evident amid this macrocosmic picture of the spread of sin with Seth, Noah, Shem, Ham, and Japheth, and this prepares the way for the microcosmic (zeroed in) focus beginning in chapter 12 on Abraham, who will bring blessing to the nations.

> ## The Big Picture

The fall initiates a downward spiral of sin, beginning with Cain's murder of Abel and culminating in the Tower of Babel.

Read through the entire text for this study, Genesis 4:1–11:26. Then interact with the following questions and record your notes on them concerning this section of Genesis. (For further background, see the *ESV Study Bible*, pages 57–70; also available online at esv.org.)

In order to get a basic snapshot of this period, skim through the following passages and jot down brief answers to the following questions: How does sin spread? What is God's punishment for that sin? How do you see God's grace in this passage?

Cain and Abel (4:1–26)

How does sin spread?

What is God's punishment for the sin of Cain?

How do you see God's grace in this passage?

Noah (6:1–22)

How does sin spread?

What is God's punishment for the sin described there?

How do you see God's grace in this passage (see also 8:20–9:7)?

Noah and his sons (9:18–29)

How does sin spread?

What is God's punishment for the sin described there?

How do you see God's grace in this passage?

The Tower of Babel (11:1–9)

How does sin spread?

What is God's punishment for the sin of building Babel?

How do you see God's grace in this passage?

Genesis is organized around sections that begin, "These are the generations of ..." (2:4; 5:1; 6:9; 10:1; 11:10, 27; 25:19; 36:1; 37:2). It is very concerned with tracing the genealogies, the offspring of Adam and Eve down through history. Look back at Genesis 3:15. Why do you think there is such a concern with genealogies that trace human offspring in the book of Genesis?

Contrast the genealogies of Cain (Gen. 4:17–24) and of Seth (4:25–5:32). What differences do you see between them? In a genealogy, the seventh and tenth generation are often significant. What do you notice about the seventh generation in each line (include Adam as the first generation)?

In Genesis 10, we see the table of nations, as the descendants from Noah spread throughout the earth. After chapter 10 the focus is on the Semites, from whom the chosen people of Israel come. But if the focus is on the line of Shem, why might Genesis 10 include accounts of all these other nations? Consider 12:1–3 as you answer.

As you think back over Genesis 4–11, what is the main point of these chapters?

Read through the following three sections on *Gospel Glimpses*, *Whole-Bible Connections*, and *Theological Soundings*. Then take time to reflect on the *Personal Implications* these sections may have for your walk with the Lord.

Gospel Glimpses

PREPARING THE WAY FOR THE GOSPEL. John the Baptist prepared the way for Jesus by saying, "Repent, for the kingdom of heaven is at hand" (Matt. 3:2). Similarly, Genesis 4–11 prepares the way for Abraham by showing the profound depths of human sinfulness when left unchecked. Dutch theologian Geerhardus Vos says that the purpose of these chapters is to "bring out the consequences of sin when left so far as possible to itself . . . . Hence, before the work of redemption is further carried out, the downward tendency of sin is clearly illustrated, in order that subsequently in the light of this downgrade movement the true divine cause of the upward course of redemption (that is, the story of Abraham and the formation of the nation Israel) might be appreciated." The ugliness and hopelessness of human sin prompt us to marvel at the even greater depths of God's love in sending his own Son to suffer on behalf of such hopeless sinners.

GRACE IN JUDGMENT. Even as God demonstrates the consequences of sin, grace abounds. Before Cain murders Abel, the Lord warns Cain about the danger of sin (Gen. 4:7). Even after that murder, God protects Cain with a mark even as he is exiled[1] from the presence of the Lord to the land of Nod, east of Eden (4:16). And when "the wickedness of man was great in the earth" (6:5), God saves Noah in an ark and resolves, "I will never again curse the ground because of man, for the intention of man's heart is evil from his youth" (8:21). Even as the LORD confuses human language at Babel and disperses them to cover the face of the earth, he does this largely to protect them from their own sin. Most importantly, throughout the downward spiral of sin evident in Genesis 4–11, God actively develops and preserves a line of holy offspring, preparing the way for the account of Abraham beginning in Genesis 12.

> ## ▶ Whole-Bible Connections

GENEALOGIES. Genesis 3:15 promised that the offspring of the woman would bruise the serpent's head. The genealogies of Genesis therefore help us trace the development of this offspring. Seth is important, since after Abel is killed and Cain exiled, we find Eve saying, "God has appointed for me another offspring instead of Abel, for Cain killed him" (Gen. 4:25). Adam was created "in the likeness of God" (5:1; cf. 1:26–27), and Adam "fathered a son in his own likeness, after his image, and named him Seth" (5:3). This image is then passed down through the blessed line of Seth in Genesis 5. The seventh generation in the blessed offspring of Seth is Enoch, who "walked with God, and he was not, for God took him" (5:24). The tenth generation is Noah, who "shall bring us relief from our work and from the painful toil of our hands" (v. 29). In contrast, the seventh generation in the offspring of Cain is Lamech, who multiplies the sin of Cain (4:23–24). In genealogical accounts the number of generations is significant; Matthew's Gospel records three sets of fourteen generations, which are six sets of seven generations. As a result, Jesus is the seventh set of generations. The line of Adam through Seth culminates in Jesus.

THE NATIONS. God originally commanded Adam, made in God's own image, to "be fruitful and multiply and fill the earth" as images and representatives of God. Instead of Adam thus filling the earth with the image of God, "the earth was corrupt in God's sight, and the earth was filled with violence" in Noah's day (Gen. 6:11). Instead of multiplying representatives of God to fill the earth, God scatters rebels against God at Babel and "dispersed them over the face of all the earth" (11:9) with many different languages. The scattering of Babel into many languages is reversed, however, at Pentecost, when God unites "devout men from every nation under heaven" in Jerusalem (Acts 2:5) to hear "in [their] own tongues the mighty works of God" (2:11).

EXILE. The consequence of sin is exile. First, Adam and Eve are sent "out from the garden of Eden" (Gen. 3:23–24). Then Cain is sent "away from the presence of the LORD and settled in the land of Nod, east of Eden" (Gen. 4:16). After the Tower of Babel is destroyed, "the LORD dispersed them over the face of all the earth" (Gen. 11:9). Jacob must similarly flee the Promised Land because of his deception and stealing of his brother's birthright, and he lives in exile with his father Laban for many years (Genesis 28–30). Even before Israel enters the Promised Land, they are warned that disobedience would lead to their exile from the land (Lev. 26:33; Deut. 28:64; 30:3–4). And Israel's sin does indeed cause them to be exiled from the land, first to Assyria and then to Babylon. However, even prophecies of the exile look forward to restoration from exile (Lev. 26:44–45; Deut. 30:3). Jesus himself is exiled to Egypt to flee the wrath of Herod (Matt. 2:13), and ultimately he experiences exile at the cross, where he cries out, "My God, my God, why have you forsaken me?" (27:46). This was an exile from the Father. The Son became sin for us, at the Father's will, so that "in him we might become the righteousness of God" (2 Cor. 5:21).

Theological Soundings

SIN. The effects of sin are not only personal but spread quickly to fill the earth. Sin is contagious. It not only affects the individual but has cosmic and corporate implications. God brought the flood because "the earth was corrupt in God's sight" (Gen. 6:11). Similarly, "the whole creation has been groaning together in the pains of childbirth until now" (Rom. 8:22). The scope of redemption is also cosmic and not only individual, as "the creation itself will be set free from its bondage to corruption," but this cosmic redemption is intertwined with the redemption of humanity since the creation will "obtain the freedom of the glory of the children of God" (8:21).

COMMON GRACE. Even as rebellion spreads throughout the earth, we see evidence of God's common grace at work. Culture develops. From Cain's line, Jubal fathered those who played the lyre and pipe, and Tubal-Cain forged instruments of bronze and iron (Gen. 4:20–22). One day, in the restored new earth, "the kings of the earth will bring their glory into it [God's city]"—that is, "the glory and the honor of the nations" (Rev. 21:24, 26).

GRACE IN RE-CREATION. Just as God created the heavens and the earth from the chaos of the waters (Gen. 1:1–2), so God initiates a work of re-creation through the waters of the flood. God makes a covenant with Noah with the sign of the rainbow after the flood (9:8–17). Just as God blessed Adam and said, "Be fruitful and multiply and fill the earth" (1:28), so God blesses Noah and says, "Be fruitful and multiply and fill the earth" (9:1, 7). Tragically, however, God's work of re-creation concludes with human rebellion once more; just as Adam sinned in the garden of Eden, so Noah sins in the garden of his vineyard (9:20–21).

Personal Implications

Take some time to reflect on the personal implications of Genesis 4:1–11:16 for your life today. Jot down your reflections under the three headings we have considered and on the passage as a whole:

1. Gospel Glimpses

2. Whole-Bible Connections

3. Theological Soundings

4. Genesis 4:1–11:16: How have you seen the progress of sin in and around your own life?

As You Finish This Unit . . .

Pray that God would seal the insights that you have obtained about the downward spiral of sin in you or your family. Ask God to uncover areas of your own heart where sin may have initiated a destructive downward spiral. Pray that the riches of the gospel might bring victory in your life as you move forward.

Definitions

[1] **Exile** – The relocation of a group of people from a preferred homeland. Several relocations of large groups of Israelites/Jews have occurred throughout history, but "the exile" typically refers to the Babylonian exile, that is, Nebuchadnezzar's relocation of residents of the southern kingdom of Judah to Babylon in 586 BC (Residents of the northern kingdom of Israel had been resettled by Assyria in 722 BC). After Babylon came under Persian rule, several waves of Jewish exiles returned and repopulated Judah.

WEEK 5: ABRAHAM AND THE NATIONS

Genesis 11:27–16:16

The Place of the Passage

We move from the macrocosmic picture of the nations in Genesis 4–11 to the microcosmic story of one man, Abram (not yet re-named Abraham), and his family, beginning in Genesis 12. Yet the wide-angle picture of all nations is not lost in the story of Abram, since God promises to bless all nations through Abram's offspring. In this section of Genesis, God makes a covenant[1] with Abram and his descendants, a covenant that is not deserved by or based on Abraham's faithfulness. It is a covenant that God himself guarantees.

The Big Picture

God promises to bless the nations through the offspring of Abram.

Read through the entire text for this study, Genesis 11:27–16:16. Then interact with the following questions and record your notes on them concerning this section of Genesis. (For further background, see the *ESV Study Bible*, pages 70–79; also available online at esv.org.)

Genesis 11:27 begins a new section: "Now these are the generations of Terah." The story of Terah, Abram's father, is told in the life of his son, Abram. Terah begins a journey to Canaan but settles in Haran (11:31). Genesis 12:1 begins, "Now the LORD said to Abram, 'Go from your country and your kindred and your father's house to the land that I will show you.'" What are the ways that God promises to bless Abram in Genesis 12:1–3?

What is ironic about God's promise to make Abram's name great (Gen. 12:2) in light of the sin at the Tower of Babel in 11:4? What are some other contrasts you see between the call of Abram and the Tower of Babel?

Abram steps out in immediate obedience. At seventy-five years of age, he takes his entire family and sets out to go to the land of Canaan. How does God confirm his promise to Abram in 12:4–9?

Despite Abram's faithful obedience in Genesis 12:4–9, his own faithlessness in 12:10–20 threatens the fulfillment of the promise. When famine strikes Egypt (12:10), Abram lies to Pharaoh about his wife Sarai (12:11–20). How does this jeopardize the fulfillment of God's promise, "To your offspring I will give this land" (12:7)? How does God intervene to ensure that his promises in these verses are fulfilled?

After Abram's "exile" in Egypt, he demonstrates more faith in his relationship with Lot in Genesis 13:1–14:16. When the land cannot support both him and Lot, he allows Lot to choose whichever land he might want (13:8–13). And when Lot is taken captive in a war by the kings of that area, Abram goes to rescue him (14:12–16). How does the Lord affirm Abram's faith and his own promises in 13:1–14:16?

Read Genesis 14:17–24. Abram meets both Melchizedek, king of Salem, and the king of Sodom. How is Abram's faith[2] demonstrated in this passage?

Genesis 15:6 is one of the best known verses in the story of Abraham: "And he believed the LORD, and he counted it to him as righteousness." While Jews around the time of Jesus generally celebrated Abram's act of sacrifice of Isaac as the pinnacle of his faith, the New Testament focuses on Abram's belief in God's promise (Rom. 4:1–25; Gal. 3:1–9). Ironically, though, the context preceding 15:6 focuses on God's promise in the face of Abram's faithlessness! How is Abram's faithlessness evident in 15:1–5?

In Genesis 15:17, a smoking fire pot passes between the pieces of Abram's sacrifice. This is an odd scene! Covenants are usually accompanied with a sacrifice, and after the covenant is sealed, each of the parties would pass between the parts of the carcass of the sacrificed animal. Walking between the parts of the carcass is like saying, "Let it be done to me if I do not fulfill my part of the covenant" (cf. Jer. 34:18–20). If fire and smoke represent the presence of God (e.g., Ex. 19:18; see also Ex. 3:2; 13:21–22), then only God and not Abram passes between the pieces of the sacrifice. What does this imply about God's commitment to keeping the terms of this covenant?

Abram's remarkable encounter with God in Genesis 15 has not cured his faithlessness. What consequences does Abram's faithless inability to trust God for the fulfillment of the promise have in Genesis 16:1–16?

Look back over 12–16. How do these chapters show God's commitment to his promise even in the face of human faithlessness?

Read through the following three sections on *Gospel Glimpses*, *Whole-Bible Connections*, and *Theological Soundings*. Then take time to reflect on the *Personal Implications* these sections may have for your walk with the Lord.

Gospel Glimpses

SACRIFICE AND THE COVENANT. God's radical commitment to his promise and covenant with Abraham is seen as he passes alone through the pieces of the sacrifice in Genesis 15:17. If the terms of the covenant are not kept, then he will bring upon himself the curses of the covenant. This radical commitment to the covenant looks forward to Christ, who took upon himself the curse of the covenant: "Christ redeemed us from the curse of the law by becoming a curse for us—for it is written, 'Cursed is everyone who is hanged on a tree'—so that in Christ Jesus the blessing of Abraham might come to the Gentiles, so that we might receive the promised Spirit through faith" (Gal. 3:13–14). Jesus has taken the curse of disobedience upon himself so that the nations might receive the blessing of Abraham.

FAITH. "And he believed the LORD, and he counted it to him as righteousness" (Gen. 15:6). When Paul celebrates salvation by faith, he looks back to Abram's faith in Genesis 15:6. In Paul's day, the Jews looked to Abraham because of his obedience in being willing to sacrifice Isaac. The focus is on Abram's obedience. The New Testament writers, however, focus more on Abram's trusting faith in Genesis 15:6 (Rom. 4:1–8; Gal. 3:1–14), and even references to the sacrifice of Isaac focus on his faith ("By *faith* Abraham, when he was tested, offered up Isaac" (Heb. 11:17). Even in Genesis, God's blessing and promise do not flow out of Abram's obedience. Rather, Abram's faith and obedience are a response to God's lavish promises. Abraham should be seen and celebrated as the father of faith.

Whole-Bible Connections

OFFSPRING OF ABRAHAM. Earlier in Genesis, God promised that the offspring of the woman would crush the head of the offspring of the serpent (Gen. 3:15). God then promises to bless the offspring of Abraham. He says, "In you all the families of the earth shall be blessed" (Gen. 12:3), and "To your offspring I will give this land" (Gen. 12:7; 15:18). In Jesus' day, the Jews claim to be legitimate offspring of Abraham—but Jesus says that they are of the devil (John 8:39–44). The apostle Paul clarifies that we are offspring of Abraham not by bloodline but by "faith line," connecting this explicitly to Genesis 12:

> Know then that it is those of faith who are the sons of Abraham. And the Scripture, foreseeing that God would justify the Gentiles by faith, preached the gospel beforehand to Abraham, saying, "In you shall all the nations be blessed." So then, those who are of faith are blessed along with Abraham, the man of faith. (Gal. 3:7–9)

Paul then clarifies that this biblical, God-spoken promise "does not say, 'And to offsprings,' referring to many, but referring to one, 'And to your offspring,' who is Christ" (Gal. 3:16). Jesus Christ ultimately fulfills God's promise to bless the nations in the offspring of Abraham. However, this blessing is not fulfilled only in Christ as an individual, for "as many of you as were baptized into Christ have put on Christ. . . . And if you are Christ's, then you are Abraham's offspring, heirs according to promise" (Gal. 3:27, 29).

EXILE TO EGYPT. Egypt plays a critical role in the story of Abraham. When famine strikes the land of Canaan, Abram immediately flees to Egypt (Gen. 12:10) and then returns to the land of Canaan. This pattern of exile and return foreshadows Israel's later slavery and affliction in Egypt (15:13), as the family of Jacob moves there so that Egypt becomes a womb for the multiplication and increase of Israel as a nation (Ex. 1:7). However, the womb of Egypt becomes a place of affliction (Ex. 1:8–14) and an "iron furnace" (Deut. 4:20), and God leads them out of Egypt back to the Promised Land. Later, Egypt becomes a metaphor for Israel's exile in Assyria: "They [Israel] shall not remain in the land of the LORD, but Ephraim shall return to Egypt, and they shall eat unclean food in Assyria" (Hos. 9:3). Historically, Israel never was exiled to Egypt after Hosea's day, but Egypt is a metaphor for their affliction and hardship. Exile is not the last word, however, since "When Israel was a child, I loved him, and out of Egypt I called my son" (Hos. 11:1), just as Hosea looks forward to the day when "they [Israel] shall come trembling like birds from Egypt, and like doves from the land of Assyria, and I will return them to their homes" (Hos. 11:11). This return from exile is ultimately fulfilled in Egypt, when Jesus as a child flees to Egypt from the murderous intentions of Herod "to fulfill what the Lord had spoken by the prophet, 'Out of Egypt I called my son'" (Matt. 2:15).

▶ Theological Soundings

THE GOD OF ABRAHAM. Repeatedly in the Bible, God reveals himself as the "God of Abraham" (e.g., Ex. 3:16; 1 Chron. 29:18; Acts 3:13). This reminder establishes that God is a God who keeps his promises. God assures Isaac, "I am the God of Abraham your father. Fear not, for I am with you" (Gen. 26:24), just as God reminds Jacob, "I am the Lord, the God of Abraham your father and the God of Isaac" (28:13). Similarly, God tells Moses to encourage the people by telling them, "The LORD, the God of your fathers, the God of Abraham, the God of Isaac, and the God of Jacob, has sent me to you" (Ex. 3:15). Even Elijah called on the "LORD, God of Abraham, Isaac, and Israel" (1 Kings 18:36) when he prayed for fire to fall on his sacrifice. Throughout the Old Testament, God reminds his people that he is the "God of Abraham" who keeps his promises. This reminder of God as the living God carries over to the New Testament, where Jesus uses this as an argument for the resurrection (Mark 12:26; Luke 20:37). This God of Abraham is the living God who continues to keep his promises and even raises the dead. The story of Abraham is not primarily about his sacrificial obedience but about God's covenantal commitment to fulfill the promises he has made.

THE NATIONS. From Genesis 1, the scope of God's concern is macrocosmic: "Be fruitful and multiply and fill the earth" (Gen. 1:28). Genesis 1–11 pictures the earth being filled not with representatives of God but with rebels against God. This was clear at Babel, when God scattered people over the face of all the earth because they desired to "make a name for ourselves" (11:4). In the face of humans seeking to make a name for themselves, God himself promises to an individual, Abraham, "I . . . will bless you and make your name great, so that you will be a blessing" (12:2). The lens of Scripture zooms in from all nations in Genesis 1–11 to one man and his family in Genesis 12–50, so that this one man's family might bless all nations (12:3). Peter (Acts 3:25–26) and Paul (Gal. 3:8) identify the ingathering of the Gentiles—upon Christ's life, death, and resurrection—as the fulfillment of this promise. And in the new earth, the redeemed people of God will be "a great multitude that no one could number, from every nation, from all tribes and peoples and languages" (Rev. 7:9).

Personal Implications

Take some time to reflect on the personal implications of Genesis 11:27–16:16 for your life today. Jot down your reflections under the three headings we have considered and on the passage as a whole:

1. Gospel Glimpses

2. Whole-Bible Connections

3. Theological Soundings

4. Genesis 11:27–16:16

As You Finish This Unit . . .

Praise God for his purpose to bless the nations through the offspring of Abraham. Pray that God would seal the insights that you have obtained about God's covenant with Abraham. Since "all the promises of God find their Yes in [Christ]" (2 Cor. 1:20), consider how the promises of Abraham can be fulfilled in your life as a spiritual child of Abraham.

Definitions

[1] **Covenant** – A binding agreement between two parties, typically involving a formal statement of their relationship, a list of stipulations and obligations for both parties, a list of witnesses to the agreement, and a list of curses for unfaithfulness and blessings for faithfulness to the agreement. The OT is more properly understood as the old covenant, meaning the agreement established between God and his people prior to the coming of Jesus Christ and the establishment of the new covenant (NT).

[2] **Faith** – Trust in or reliance upon something or someone despite a lack of concrete proof. Salvation, which is purely a work of God's grace, can be received only through faith (Rom. 5:2; Eph. 2:8–9). The writer of Hebrews calls on believers to emulate those who lived godly lives by faith (Hebrews 11).

Week 6: Promises Fulfilled

Genesis 17:1–22:24

The Place of the Passage

God promises that Abram, now re-named Abraham, will be "the father of a multitude of nations" (Gen. 17:5). God calls Abraham to "walk before me, and be blameless, that I may make my covenant between me and you, and may multiply you greatly" (vv. 1–2). God's intention to bless the nations through Abraham is evident throughout this section as Abraham intercedes for Sodom and Gomorrah and brings blessing to the Philistine king Abimelech. Also, we see both the miraculous birth of Isaac and later Abraham's offering of Isaac. Throughout, God's faithfulness is clear.

The Big Picture

God fulfills his promises and hears the prayers of his people.

> ## Reflection and Discussion

Read through the entire text for this study, Genesis 17:1–22:24. Then interact with the following questions and record your notes on them concerning this section of Genesis. (For further background, see the *ESV Study Bible*, pages 79–88; also available online at esv.org.)

Covenant and Circumcision

God reiterates his covenant promises to Abraham in Genesis 17:3–8. These promises revolve around the blessings of offspring, land, and God's presence. In terms of offspring, God promises, "I will make you exceedingly fruitful, and I will make you into nations, and kings shall come from you" (17:6). For the land, "I will give to you and to your offspring after you the land of your sojournings, all the land of Canaan, for an everlasting possession" (17:8). God's presence is promised, since "I will be their God" (17:8). God's promise demands a response—circumcision.[1] Read 17:9–14 carefully. Since God's promises revolve around the promise of offspring, why do you think this sign is chosen as a sign of the covenant? In what ways is this sign uniquely appropriate?

God changes Abram's name to Abraham (meaning "exalted father"), and he changes Sarai's name to Sarah. God then reiterates his promise to bless Sarah and bring a child from her womb. Read Genesis 17:15–21; 18:9–15. How do you see Abraham and Sarah's incredulity in the face of God's promise?

Even in the face of his incredulity, Abraham still responds to God's promise with obedience and circumcises his son Ishmael and the men born in his house. Notice that the covenant of circumcision does not only cover his own biological children but also includes "all those born in his house or bought with his money" (Gen. 17:23). How might this begin to reflect God's promise that "in you all the families of the earth shall be blessed" (12:3)?

Abraham and the Nations

God's purpose for the nations continues to be seen in the second half of Genesis 18. In verses 1–8, the Lord appears to Abraham with three men, and Abraham immediately responds with generous hospitality to them. After reiterating his promise in Gen. 18:9–15, God's judgment is sure against Sodom and Gomorrah (v. 20). But Abraham seeks to bring blessing to these nations by interceding[2] for them (vv. 22–33), a back and forth conversation between the Lord and Abraham. We clearly see Abraham's persistence here, asking six times for God to lower the threshold for his judgment. Abraham's relationship with God allows him to ask questions of God and shows a remarkable persistence. What lessons can we learn about the nature of prayer from this? Why is it important to have an "Abraham" type figure to intercede in the face of God's judgment?

Read the description of the remarkable sinfulness of Sodom and Gomorrah in Genesis 19:1–11. In light of this, Lot leaves Sodom with his immediate family in 19:12–29, though his sons-in-law do not believe in the impending destruction. They flee to the city of Zoar, and the Lord rains down sulfur and fire from heaven to destroy the cities and the valley they have left behind. Lot's wife turns back during this time of destruction and is turned into a pillar of salt. Read this section carefully. Why do you think this story is included in the overall story of Abraham? How does this help us understand the promise, "In you all the families of the earth shall be blessed"?

The problems of the nations do not end with the destruction of Sodom and Gomorrah. How do we see the questionable origins of the Ammonites and Moabites in Genesis 19:30–38?

Again, we see Abraham's interactions with the nations in Genesis 20. How does he bring blessing to the Philistines, even though he lies about the identity of his wife? Note also 21:22–34. What do we learn about Abraham and about the nature of sin when we compare 20:1–18 with 12:10–20?

Promise Fulfilled and Tested

In Genesis 21:1–7, Isaac is finally born. After waiting twenty-five years, Abraham is given a son. What irony can be seen in the name of Isaac, "he laughs"?

Now that Isaac is born, conflict arises with Ishmael, the son of Hagar. Sarah in particular tells her husband, "Cast out this slave woman with her son" (Gen. 21:10). God promises Abraham, even in the midst of his displeasure and frustration, that "I will make a nation of the son of the slave woman also, because he is your offspring" (v. 13). Observe carefully what happens to Hagar as she is sent away. How does Genesis 21:8–20 show God's blessing resting on Ishmael and his descendants because of Abraham?

A final step of painful obedience is seen in Genesis 22:1–24. "God tested Abraham" (22:1). This sets the tone for the entire chapter, as God calls him to "Take your son, your only son Isaac, whom you love, and go to the land of Moriah, and offer him there as a burnt offering on one of the mountains of which I shall tell you" (22:2). This test is painful, but Abraham obeys immediately. Read through Gen. 22:1–8. How do you see Abraham taking deliberate steps of trusting obedience here? Note the way the covenant promises to Abraham are reiterated in verses 15–18.

Read through the following three sections on *Gospel Glimpses*, *Whole-Bible Connections*, and *Theological Soundings*. Then take time to reflect on the *Personal Implications* these sections may have for your walk with the Lord.

▶ Gospel Glimpses

INTERCESSION/INTERMEDIARY. As God reveals his impending judgment upon Sodom and Gomorrah, Abraham steps in as an interceder and intermediary. Six times he comes before God and intercedes on behalf of those cities. Similarly, when Israel sinned by making a golden calf and God was going to destroy them completely, Moses interceded for them, saying, "But now, if you will forgive their sin—but if not, please blot me out of your book that you have written" (Ex. 32:32). He stood "in the breach" (Ezek. 22:30) and cried out for God's grace for Israel just as Abraham did for Sodom and Gomorrah. Paul too cried out in his own day on behalf of the Israelites, "I could wish that I myself were accursed and cut off from Christ for the sake of my brothers, my kinsmen according to the flesh" (Rom. 9:3). All these serve to point to Jesus, the ultimate intercessor and intermediary, who stood in the breach for us—he "redeemed us from the curse of the law by becoming a curse for us" (Gal. 3:13).

SACRIFICE OF ISAAC, SACRIFICE OF JESUS. The sacrifice of Isaac looks forward to the sacrifice of Jesus Christ. God commands Abraham, "Take your son, your *only son* Isaac, whom you *love*, and . . . offer him there as a burnt offering" (Gen. 22:2). This wording foreshadows the words in John's Gospel, "For God so *loved* the world, that he gave his *only Son*, that whoever believes in him should not perish but have eternal life" (John 3:16). Also, God commends Abraham, because "you have not withheld your son, your only son, from me" (Gen. 22:12), just as he himself "did not spare his own Son but gave him up for us all" (Rom 8:32). Abraham prepares to sacrifice his only beloved son, Isaac, but a ram is provided instead. Ultimately, however, God actually does offer his only, beloved Son as a sacrifice for us.

Whole-Bible Connections

CIRCUMCISION. The mark of the covenant of Abraham was circumcision. Circumcision is a picture of the need for cleansing. When Israel crosses the Jordan to enter the Promised Land in Joshua's day, a whole generation is circumcised. When that is done, the Lord declares, "Today I have rolled away the reproach of Egypt from you" (Josh 5:9). Circumcising the foreskin is an important reminder that the offspring is blessed from generation to generation. It is not only blood children but even foreigners who are circumcised, showing God's plan from the beginning for the nations. A failure to circumcise would lead to that person being "cut off from his people" (Gen. 17:14). Circumcision is a physical branding of people as formally members of God's covenantal people, but it is meant to signify a spiritual effecting of inclusion among the people of God; Moses tells the people, "Circumcise therefore the foreskin of your heart" (Deut. 10:16). God promises that after the exile, "the LORD your God will circumcise your heart and the heart of your offspring" (Deut. 30:6). Physical circumcision alone is not enough (cf. Jer. 9:25–26), and the circumcised Jews in Jesus' day are "uncircumcised in heart and ears" (Acts 7:51). Paul underscores that circumcision is meant to signify inner spiritual renewal, so that the presence of physical circumcision in the absence of spiritual circumcision is of no benefit at all (Rom. 2:25–29).

TESTING. By asking him to sacrifice his beloved and only son Isaac, "God *tested* Abraham" (Gen. 22:1). This testing is not unique to Abraham. Later, God led Israel for forty years in the wilderness "that he might humble you, *testing* you to know what was in your heart, whether you would keep his commandments or not" (Deut. 8:2). God tested Israel to show them the reality of their heart, so that they might learn humble dependence on God's provision and that "man does not live by bread alone, but . . . by every word that comes from the mouth of the LORD" (Deut. 8:3). Israel, of course, failed their test in the wilderness, and this point is underscored in Deuteronomy 6–8. Jesus similarly is tested and tried in the wilderness, and Jesus is found faithful where Israel failed. Jesus' faithfulness in the place of Israel's failure is underscored as Jesus quotes from Deuteronomy 6–8 at his temptation (Matt. 4:1–11). We who believe in Jesus are also tested with hardships: "Beloved, do not be surprised at the fiery trial when it comes upon you to test you. . . . But rejoice insofar as you share Christ's sufferings" (1 Pet. 4:12–13). Even our failings as God's children in our testings, however, need not throw us into despair, for Jesus has passed the ultimate test on our behalf.

Theological Soundings

JUDGMENT. God's judgment upon Sodom and Gomorrah becomes a picture of the totality and severity of God's judgment throughout the Bible (e.g., Deut. 29:23; Isa. 1:9; Jer. 23:14; 50:40; Amos 4:11). God compares rebellious Israel to Sodom, who "had pride, excess of food, and prosperous ease, but did not aid the poor and needy" (Ezek. 16:49). Jesus looks back to the judgment on Sodom and Gomorrah and says that the sin of those who rejected him would be even greater: "I tell you that it will be more tolerable on the day of judgment for the land of Sodom than for you" (Matt. 11:24; Luke 10:12). God is unswervingly just. Every evil deed will either be paid for by Christ's sacrifice or punished personally and eternally in hell.

EVERLASTING GOD. In Genesis 17, God makes an "everlasting covenant" with Abraham (Gen. 17:7), marked by the sign of circumcision. Also, after the birth of Isaac and the treaty with Abimelech, Abraham plants a tree at Beersheba and "called there on the name of the Lord, the Everlasting God" (21:33). After waiting twenty-five years, Abraham sees the promise fulfilled and experiences God's provision and protection time and again. As a result, he calls on the name of the LORD, who is the everlasting God. He does not change over time. His promises are everlasting and trustworthy.

Personal Implications

Take some time to reflect on the personal implications of Genesis 17:1–22:24 for your life today. Jot down your reflections under the three headings we have considered and on the passage as a whole:

1. Gospel Glimpses

2. Whole-Bible Connections

3. Theological Soundings

4. Genesis 17:1–22:24

As You Finish This Unit . . .

Praise God for his heart for the nations and commitment to his promises. Pray that God would keep you strong in the place of your testing. Write down some notes or questions for further reflection below.

Definitions

[1] **Circumcision** – The ritual practice of removing the foreskin of an individual, which was commanded for all male Israelites in OT times as a sign of participation in the covenant God established with Abraham (Gen. 17:9–14).

[2] **Intercession** – Appealing to one person on behalf of another, often used with reference to prayer.

Week 7: Passing the Promises from Abraham to Isaac

Genesis 23:1–26:33

In this section, the torch of God's promise is passed from Abraham to Isaac. In the closing days of Abraham's life, Sarah dies, and Abraham turns his attention to finding a wife for his son Isaac. The story of Abraham continues in the account of Isaac and the birth of his sons, Esau and Jacob. God's promises are reiterated to Isaac, just as they were previously to Abraham. Isaac not only receives the promises of God to Abraham but also inherits some of the same foibles, as we will see. In this section, we want to focus on how the promises to Abraham are passed down to the next generation. God is preserving an offspring (Gen. 3:15).

The Big Picture

At the twilight of Abraham's life, he passes down the torch of his faith to Isaac.

> ### Reflection and Discussion

Read through the entire text for this study, Genesis 23:1–26:33. Then interact with the following questions and record your notes on them concerning this section of Genesis. (For further background, see the *ESV Study Bible*, pages 89–96; also available online at esv.org.)

Passing the Torch by Preserving the Line (Genesis 23–24)

Genesis 23–24 is a picture of transition. Chapter 23 captures the scene of Sarah's death. Chapter 24 opens with Abraham aging (Gen. 24:1). He wants his son not to marry a Canaanite but a woman from his own country (24:3–4). Why is the matter of a wife for Isaac such a matter of grave concern for Abraham (cf. Deut. 7:3–4)?

What is the significance of the location of Sarah's burial? Consider God's promises such as Genesis 12:1, 7; 13:15; 15:18; 17:8.

Read through chapter 24. How do the details of this story confirm Abraham's confidence that "the LORD, the God of heaven . . . will send his angel[1] before you, and you shall take a wife for my son from there" (Gen. 24:7)? Note again Abraham's concern about intermarriage.[2]

Passing the Torch from Abraham to Isaac (Genesis 25–26)

A new section begins in Genesis 25:19. In what ways do you see the faith of Abraham passed on to Isaac in verses 19–26? Observe, among other things, also how long it takes for Isaac to have his first son (see vv. 20, 26).

Conflict sets the stage for the story of Isaac. Jacob is born grasping the heel of his brother Esau, and so is named "Jacob" (lit., "he cheats"). Division between the brothers is clear from birth, and Isaac favors Esau while Rebekah favors Jacob. How does Gen. 25:29–34 underscore the appropriateness of Jacob's name?

Read Genesis 26:1–16. Immediately after God confirms his covenant promises to Isaac (26:3–4), Isaac utters the exact same lie about his wife that his father did—even in the same place (Gerar) with the same king (Abimelech;

see Genesis 20). Nevertheless the Lord blesses Isaac abundantly in that land. He has so many possessions that the Philistines envy him! Why do you think this account of blessing (26:12–16) is juxtaposed with the account of Isaac's deception (vv. 7–11)? What does this suggest about the nature of God's blessing in our lives?

Read Genesis 26:17–33. The focus here is how Isaac moves about and digs the wells that Abraham had dug. This is not merely about water. It is about something more, since Isaac gives them the names that his father had given them. In particular, Beersheba is dug with remarkable similarities to how it was originally dug in Abraham's time (Gen. 21:22–33). God has promised Isaac that "in your offspring all the nations of the earth shall be blessed" (26:4). How is this seen in these verses?

Read through the following three sections on *Gospel Glimpses*, *Whole-Bible Connections*, and *Theological Soundings*. Then take time to reflect on the *Personal Implications* these sections may have for your walk with the Lord.

▶ Gospel Glimpses

PRAYER AND PROVISION. Throughout this section, we see how God provides in response to prayer. The servant's prayer for finding a wife for Isaac (Gen.

24:12) is answered, and the servant celebrates: "Blessed be the LORD, the God of my master Abraham, who has not forsaken his steadfast love and his faithfulness toward my master" (24:27). Isaac's prayer for his barren wife Rebekah is answered so that she conceives (25:21). Indeed, the God who cares for the lilies of the field and the birds of the air cares for his children as well (Matt. 6:26–29). God's fatherly care is ultimately seen in the gift of his Son. This gift reminds us, "He who did not spare his own Son but gave him up for us all, how will he not also with him graciously give us all things?" (Rom 8:32). The gospel shows that God cares intensely even for the personal needs of his people, and that in his Son's work any reason for God to resist hearing us has been swept away. We can come before him boldly in prayer.

"I AM WITH YOU." God appears to Isaac as he settles in Gerar, and God appears to him at Beersheba to remind him, "I am the God of Abraham your father. Fear not, *for I am with you* and will bless you and multiply your offspring for my servant Abraham's sake" (Gen. 26:24). Similarly, God calls Moses to lead Israel out of slavery, assuring him that, "I AM WHO I AM," and, "The Lord, the God of your fathers, the God of Abraham, of Isaac, and of Jacob . . . will bring you up out of the affliction of Egypt" (Ex. 3:14–17). When God's people are under threat, God gives a sign to Ahaz that "the virgin shall conceive and bear a son, and shall call his name Immanuel" (Isa. 7:14), which means "God is with us." God's presence is assured during the exile, just as God assured Isaac of his presence in his exile in Gerar and Moses in Midian. Ultimately, Jesus manifests God's presence with us to save us from our sins, fulfilling the prophecy of Isaiah 7:14 (Matt. 1:21–23). Indeed, in Jesus, "the Word became flesh and dwelt among us" (John 1:14).

> ### Whole-Bible Connections

BARRENNESS. The fall brought "pain in childbearing" to women (Gen. 3:16). This consequence is filled out throughout Genesis as the wives of the patriarchs are afflicted with barrenness: Sarah (11:30), Rebekah (25:21), and Rachel (29:31). Throughout Scripture, the pain of barrenness is also seen with the wife of Manoah (Judges 13), with Hannah (1 Samuel 1–2), the Shunammite woman (2 Kings 4:8–17), and Elizabeth (Luke 1). Barrenness is not the direct result of sin. Nevertheless, in these cases God brought it about (Gen. 16:2; 30:2; 1 Sam. 1:5) to accomplish a divine purpose. God not only closes the womb but opens it, and some of the most important heroes in history are born from such formerly barren woman (Isaac, Jacob, Joseph, Samson, Samuel, and John the Baptist). As a result, barrenness is not a cause for despair but for expectation; Isaiah calls out, "Sing, O barren one, who did not bear. . . . For the children of the desolate one will be more than the children of her who is married" (Isa. 54:1).

INTERMARRIAGE. Abraham focuses on getting a wife for Isaac from his own country and kindred (Gen. 24:4). The problem of intermarriage is highlighted by Esau's marriage to Hittite women who "made life bitter for Isaac and Rebekah" (Gen. 26:35). The concern here is not simply familial but spiritual. The danger of intermarriage is that it would lead the hearts of Israel towards idolatry[3] (Ex. 34:16; Deut. 7:3–4). Intermarriage leads to idolatry during the period of the Judges (Judg. 3:6; 14:3) as well as with Solomon (1 Kings. 11:1–2). As a result, the discovery of intermarriage after the exile is a matter of grave concern for Ezra and Nehemiah (Ezra 10; Neh. 13:23–27). The post-exilic prophet Malachi continues to lament, "Judah has profaned the sanctuary of the LORD, which he loves, and has married the daughter of a foreign god" (Mal. 2:11). In a similar vein, Paul insists that Christians should not marry non-Christians (2 Cor. 6:14–18).

Theological Soundings

GOD OF ABRAHAM AND ISAAC. God does not change. The God who has promised and revealed himself to Abraham now extends those same promises and revelation to Isaac. God appears to him at Beersheba and assures him, "I am the God of Abraham your father" who "will bless you and multiply your offspring for my servant Abraham's sake" (Gen. 26:24). Even as Isaac faces the same challenges that Abraham did in famine (26:1), God appears and leads him in specific ways. Throughout the Bible, God will reveal himself as the "God of Abraham, Isaac and Jacob." He is a self-consistent, utterly reliable God.

STEADFAST LOVE. God's steadfast love is evident throughout this passage. When the servant looks for a wife for Isaac, he pleads for "steadfast love to my master Abraham" (Gen. 24:12). When his prayer is answered, he celebrates: "Blessed be the LORD, the God of my master Abraham, who has not forsaken his steadfast love and his faithfulness toward my master" (24:27). Abraham does nothing to deserve this steadfast love, but God's character is demonstrated in the grace that abounds in Abraham's life. While God has bound himself to his people by formal covenant, the steadfast love that binds him to his people, which the covenant expresses, issues forth from his very heart. He *is* love (1 John 4:8). He is "the God of all grace" (1 Pet. 5:10).

Personal Implications

Take some time to reflect on the personal implications of Genesis 23:1–26:33 for your life today. Jot down your reflections under the three headings we have considered and on the passage as a whole:

1. Gospel Glimpses

2. Whole-Bible Connections

3. Theological Soundings

4. Genesis 23:1–26:33

▶ **As You Finish This Unit . . .**

Praise God for how the promises and blessings of Abraham are passed on to his son Isaac and to all the offspring of Isaac, including us. What aspects of the promise stand out to you? What convictions is God laying on your heart through this study? Respond to God in a moment of unhurried prayer.

Definitions

[1] **Angel** – A supernatural messenger of God, often sent to carry out his will or to assist human beings in carrying out his will. Though angels are more powerful than humans and often instill awe, they are not to be worshiped (Col. 2:18; Rev. 22:8–9). The Bible does, however, note various appearances of an "angel of the Lord," apparently a visible manifestation of God himself.

[2] **Intermarriage** – Marriage between a man and a woman of different ethnicity. In the Old Testament, intermarriage often led to spiritual compromise.

[3] **Idolatry** – In the Bible, idolatry usually refers to the worship of a physical object instead of the true God. Paul's comments in Colossians 3:5, however, suggest that idolatry can include covetousness, since to covet is essentially to worship material things.

Week 8: Lessons from Deception

Genesis 26:34—31:55

The Place of the Passage

In the previous section, we saw that the promises of God to Abraham are passed on to Isaac. However, the story of Isaac is ultimately told in the life of his son Jacob. Jacob's grasping at birth (Gen. 25:26) and manipulating of his brother Esau (vv. 29–34) foreshadow the outright deception that Jacob engages in to steal Esau's birthright in Genesis 27. This section traces the consequences of Jacob's deception in his exile to Laban's country, as Jacob the deceiver is deceived and the manipulator is manipulated.

The Big Picture

Sinful deception banishes Jacob into personal exile, but the punishment of sin prepares Jacob for his encounter with God at Bethel and beyond.

> ### Reflection and Discussion

Read through the entire text for this study, Genesis 26:34–31:55. Then interact with the following questions and record your notes on them concerning this section of Genesis. (For further background, see the *ESV Study Bible*, pages 96–106; also available online at esv.org.)

The Deception

Genesis 27:1 begins, "When Isaac was old and his eyes were dim so that he could not see . . ." In the Bible, dim eyesight can refer not only to physical eyesight but also spiritual discernment (e.g., 1 Sam. 3:1–2), while undimmed eyesight may symbolize physical and spiritual vigor (e.g., Deut. 34:7). In light of these other passages, it seems that Isaac's dim eyes may be not only physical but also spiritual. When "Abraham was old, well advanced in years" (Gen. 24:1) his concern was singularly focused on providing a proper spouse for Isaac. What evidences are there for Isaac's lack of spiritual discernment in Genesis 26:34–27:4?

Read the story of Jacob and Rebekah's deception of Isaac in order for Jacob to get his blessing in Genesis 27:5–27:46. While the deception succeeds, by the end of the chapter it is clear that everybody loses. Isaac's spiritual blurriness leads to painful consequences for his entire family. Note the painful consequences that are experienced by:

Isaac:

Esau:

_____

_____

_____

_____

_____

Jacob:

_____

_____

_____

_____

_____

Rebekah:

_____

_____

_____

_____

_____

What evidences do you see throughout Genesis 28 of God confirming to Jacob the same covenant promises made to his father, Isaac, and his grandfather, Abraham?

_____

_____

_____

_____

_____

For his deception, Jacob must go into "exile" to the land of Laban because his brother desires to kill him (Gen. 27:42–45; 28:5). Jacob's encounter with God at Bethel propels him forward in obedience in Genesis 29:1–14. Unlike the deceiving and manipulating Jacob of the past, he shows generosity (29:10) and candor to his uncle Laban (29:13). However, in exile in the land of Laban, Jacob the deceiver feels the pain of deception in 29:15–30. Read that story. How does Jacob's declaration to Laban, "Why then have you deceived me?" (29:25) ironically echo Isaac's declaration to Esau in 27:35? What might God be teaching Jacob through the pain of this situation?

Jacob is not only deceived but also manipulated. While Jacob should have known the pain of favoritism because of his father's favoritism toward Esau (Gen. 25:28), he shows the same favoritism toward his wife Rachel (29:30). As a result, Jacob is manipulated by his own wives repeatedly in 29:31–30:24. Describe some ways in which we see Jacob himself being manipulated.

Read about Jacob's relationship with Laban in Genesis 30:1–43. Laban tries to cheat Jacob out of his wages by removing the striped and spotted goats and black lambs from the flock. However, Jacob employs an odd mating technique that works to his favor, and he prospers. How does Jacob experience God's grace in the face of Laban's manipulative techniques here?

The Lord clearly calls Jacob to return home from his exile: "Return to the land of your fathers and to your kindred, and I will be with you" (Gen. 31:3). How are Jacob's old ways still evident as his family flees from Laban in Genesis 31:14–35?

_____

_____

_____

_____

_____

_____

Read Genesis 31:43–55 and note the reconciliation[1] between Jacob and Laban. What broken relationship still needs to be reconciled for Jacob?

_____

_____

_____

_____

_____

_____

Read through the following three sections on *Gospel Glimpses*, *Whole-Bible Connections*, and *Theological Soundings*. Then take time to reflect on the *Personal Implications* these sections may have for your walk with the Lord.

Gospel Glimpses

JUDAH AND LEVI. Leah was unloved, but God blessed her with many children. Her sons include Judah and Levi. Judah becomes the father of the royal tribe of David and ultimately Jesus, and Levi is the father of the priestly tribe, which also culminates in the true and final priest, Jesus (Heb. 7:23–28). It is surprising that both the royal and priestly lines are children of Leah, the unloved and neglected wife of Jacob. God shines the grace and power of his purposes in the most unlikely of places.

"EXILE." "The Lord disciplines the one he loves, and chastises every son whom he receives" (Heb. 12:6). Jacob experiences a painful exile from the land of Canaan because of his deception, and he must flee to the land of Laban. There, the deceiver is deceived and the manipulator is manipulated, but those twenty years of "exile" form Jacob's character and prepare him for a remarkable reconciliation with his brother Esau and with God himself. What Jacob (Israel) experiences individually through repentance and restoration through exile, God prophecies would happen to Israel corporately after exile (Deut. 30:1–10). Corporate Israel experiences the pain of exile to Assyria and Babylon, but the full blessing after exile is not realized until Jesus comes. Jesus experiences temporary "exile" to Egypt (Matt. 2:13–15) and ultimate exile when he was forsaken by God on the cross (Matt. 27:46). Seeing Jesus undergo the exile from the Father that we deserve, our hearts are transformed to love him unreservedly.

Whole-Bible Connections

EYESIGHT. Just as Isaac's eyesight was "dim so that he could not see" (Gen. 27:1), so later the priest Eli's "eyesight had begun to grow dim so that he could not see" during a time when "the word of the LORD was rare . . . there was no frequent vision" (1 Sam. 3:1–2). For both Isaac and Eli, their lack of spiritual discernment affected their children. Isaac failed to get a proper wife for his son Esau, and Eli failed to teach his sons properly the ways of the priesthood (1 Sam. 2:12–17). Later, Jesus drew an analogy between physical and spiritual sight: "The eye is the lamp of the body. So, if your eye is healthy, your whole body will be full of light, but if your eye is bad, your whole body will be full of darkness. If then the light in you is darkness, how great is the darkness!" (Matt. 6:22–23).

BETHEL is a significant place in the story of Jacob. After first meeting God at Bethel, Jacob vows to return to Bethel "if God will be with me and will keep me in this way that I go" (Gen. 28:20). He is testing to see if this God is real. However, as he experiences God's provision, he sees God as "the God of Bethel" (31:13; 35:7). After his "exile" in the land of Laban for twenty years, God tells him to "return to the land of your fathers and to your kindred, and I will be with you" (31:3). In chapter 35, he finally returns to Bethel. Yet Bethel becomes the site of a rival cult to Jerusalem (1 Kings. 12:28–13:32), and Bethel becomes synonymous later with idolatry (Amos 4:4; 5:5–6; Hos. 10:15; Jer. 48:13). Ultimately, what Jacob originally saw at Bethel with angels "ascending and descending" (Gen. 28:12) to the presence of God looked forward to Jesus' promise to Nathanael that "you will see heaven opened, and the angels of God ascending and descending on the Son of Man" (John 1:51).

Theological Soundings

DISCIPLINE. God's disciplining hand is clearly upon Jacob. God's promises and purposes do not eradicate our responsibility. Even as God's promise and purpose so clearly rest upon Jacob, he still faces painful consequences of his actions in the land of Laban. Even though Christ has paid the price of our sin upon the cross, we still require the chastening of God's wise, fatherly hand to allure our hearts away from the world and toward Christ. In such times God is treating us with love—he is treating us as his own children (Heb. 12:7).

UNDESERVED BLESSING. Throughout this account, Jacob, the deceiver, is the recipient of incredibly undeserved blessing. He prospers greatly in the land of Laban, as he "increased greatly and had large flocks, female servants and male servants, and camels and donkeys" (Gen. 30:43). Jacob recognizes God's gracious hand and concludes, "If the God of my father, the God of Abraham and the Fear of Isaac, had not been on my side, surely now you would have sent me away empty-handed. God saw my affliction and the labor of my hands" (31:42).

Personal Implications

Take some time to reflect on the personal implications of Genesis 26:34–31:55 for your life today. Jot down your reflections under the three headings we have considered and on the passage as a whole:

1. Gospel Glimpses

2. Whole-Bible Connections

3. Theological Soundings

4. Genesis 26:34–31:55

> ### As You Finish This Unit . . .

Just as God disciplined Jacob in "exile" in the land of Laban, so God disciplines us for our good. How has God's disciplining hand rested on your life? How do you continue to see his discipline working out in your life? What good has emerged from that? Take some time to reflect on the nature of the Lord's discipline in your own life.

Definitions

[1] **Reconciliation** – The restoration of a positive relationship and peace between alienated or opposing parties. Through his death and resurrection, Jesus has reconciled believers to God (2 Cor. 5:18–21).

WEEK 9: FROM JACOB TO ISRAEL

Genesis 32:1–35:29

In the previous section, we saw that Jacob goes into "exile" in the land of Laban and experiences the very pain of deception that he had inflicted upon his brother Esau. During the twenty years in that land, God had worked in Jacob's heart. In this section, Jacob faces his greatest fears in reconciling with his brother Esau. As he does so, we see a dramatic picture of the grace of God through Esau.

The Big Picture

Crippled for life after wrestling with God, Jacob reconciles with Esau and finishes his journey to Bethel.

Reflection and Discussion

Read through the entire text for this study, Genesis 32:1–35:29. Then interact with the following questions and record your notes on them concerning this section of Genesis. (For further background, see the *ESV Study Bible*, pages 106–112; also available online at esv.org.)

In the opening scene of Genesis 32:1–8, Jacob is gripped with fear. To his credit, he is on the journey, on the way to the Promised Land in obedience to the word of God (31:3). Yet as he faces the prospect of seeing his brother Esau again, fear grips Jacob's heart as he hears that his brother is approaching with four hundred men. However, Jacob brings this fear before God in prayer in 32:9–12. Read this prayer carefully. What characteristics and promises of God strengthen Jacob to cast his fears upon God?

Jacob not only wrestles with God in prayer but he also wrestles with the reality of repentance.[1] Read Genesis 32:13–21. He sends a very lavish present to Esau in front of him—goats, ewes, rams, camels, cows, bulls, and donkeys. According to 32:20, the purpose of these gifts are to "appease him with the present" so that "he will accept me." This language is often used of sacrifices before God. How do these gifts reflect the reality of repentance in Jacob's life?

We see a dramatic turning point in Jacob's life in Genesis 32:22–32. He wrestles with a man, just as he has been wrestling with different situations up to this point in 32:22–24. The turning point for Jacob, though, is the confession of his weakness. In 32:27, after wrestling with God, Jacob confesses that his name is "Jacob," the cheater. In light of 27:36 ("Esau said, 'Is he not rightly named Jacob? For he has cheated me these two times. He took away my birthright, and behold, now he has taken away my blessing'"), what might be the significance of this confession? God gives Jacob a new name, Israel, meaning apparently "he strives with God." What message was there for Jacob in this new name?

_____

_____

_____

_____

_____

_____

Jacob pled with God to bless him. Was this prayer answered? If so, how?

_____

_____

_____

_____

Read Genesis 33:1–11. At first, it seems that Jacob is back to his old scheming, as he divides his family to prevent them from total slaughter (33:1–2; cf. v. 8). Yet what evidences do we see that Jacob takes responsibility and actively pursues reconciliation in these verses? List any hints you see of Jacob's heart of repentance and active pursuit of reconciliation in these verses.

_____

_____

_____

_____

_____

Though Esau had been deeply wronged and formerly wanted to kill Jacob (Gen. 27:41), we see a remarkable change in him as he "ran to meet [Jacob] and embraced him and fell on his neck and kissed him" (33:4). In 33:12–20, Esau offers to go with Jacob, or at least provide a bodyguard to be with him. Jacob refuses. God had promised him the land of Canaan and had promised to be his protection and bodyguard (31:3), so he did not need the protection of Esau. Another reason Jacob may have refused to go with Esau was that he had vowed to return to Bethel (28:20–22). God had told him to return to the land of his fathers and fulfill his vow (31:3, 13). How does all this tie in to the original promise to Abraham in 12:1 (reiterated in 13:15, 17; 15:7, 18; 17:8)?

Look carefully at Jacob's response in Genesis 34:5–7, 30–31. Jacob tends toward passivity and cowardice, as in the past. Jacob also favored Rachel over Leah, and here he favors the children of Rachel over the children of Leah, as Dinah is the daughter of Leah. How would you describe Jacob's response here? Where is his focus?

Look at the response of the sons of Jacob to this tragedy. How do their actions reflect some of the characteristics of their father (see esp. Gen. 34:13)?

In spite of the disaster of Genesis 34, God does not give up on Jacob. God reaffirms his call to Jacob in Gen. 35:1. As Jacob responds to this call in verses 2–4, what must he and his family do before they arise and go up to Bethel? What is the significance of this?

How does God confirm his promise to Jacob in Genesis 35:9–15? How does this confirmation pick up on things God has said to Abraham and Isaac, as well as on God's original words to Adam and Eve in 1:28?

Read through the following three sections on *Gospel Glimpses*, *Whole-Bible Connections*, and *Theological Soundings*. Then take time to reflect on the *Personal Implications* these sections may have for your walk with the Lord.

Gospel Glimpses

ESAU AND THE HEART OF GOD. Esau unexpectedly runs to welcome his brother Jacob, who has stolen his blessing and birthright. Though Jacob had sinned against Esau, Esau welcomes him back with open arms. Similarly, we have sinned against God, but God the Father welcomes us back with open arms. In fact, just as Esau "*ran* to meet him and *embraced* him and fell on his neck and *kissed* him, and they wept" (Gen. 33:4), so the father in the story of the prodigal son "*ran* and *embraced* him and *kissed* him" (Luke 15:20). Just as Jacob stole the father's blessing, so the prodigal son prematurely demanded the father's blessing. Just as Esau unexpectedly welcomes back the rebel Jacob, so the father unexpectedly welcomes back the son. What a beautiful picture of the gospel in an unexpected place!

RECONCILIATION. Jacob takes seriously the task of reconciliation with his brother Esau. He sends forth a sizeable present, a "blessing" (Gen. 33:11), presumably repaying the blessing that he had stolen from his brother many years earlier (27:35). When his life is realigned to God after wrestling at Peniel (32:30), this realignment with God is immediately seen in reconciliation with his brother. Similarly, when Jesus encounters Zacchaeus the tax collector, Zacchaeus immediately responds by paying back what he has stolen from others (Luke 19:8). The gospel not only reconciles us to God (Eph. 2:1–10), but also restores our relationships with one another (Eph. 2:11–22).

71

Whole-Bible Connections

SIMEON AND LEVI. Oddly enough, these two brothers play a critical role in God's plan. Although they arrange the bloodbath of the city of Shechem and are later cursed for their part in it (Gen. 49:5–7), Levi would ultimately become the father of the tribe of the priesthood of all of Israel (the Levites). Simeon is also the father of one of the major tribes of Israel.

JACOB is born a cheater (Gen. 25:26) and lives up to his name by deceiving his brother Esau for his father's blessing (27:36). Despite Jacob's unsavory character, God's undeserved blessing and promise continue to rest upon him. When he wrestles with God, confessing his name as Jacob in Genesis 32:27, God renames him Israel. Even after he receives his new name, he is still called Jacob (46:2, 5) and manifests his old character in failing to rebuke his sons for the murder of the men of the city of Shechem (Genesis 34), and in his doting on Joseph (37:3). Indeed, both the old name Jacob and new name Israel are used, even in the same verse (46:5). He is both a failure and a loved one at the same time. Generations later in the time of the prophet Hosea, rebellious Israel is called Jacob, indicted, and called to repentance (Hos. 12:2–6). For Paul, Jacob illustrates God's mercy and compassion (Rom. 9:10–16).

Theological Soundings

GOD'S STEADFAST LOVE AND FAITHFULNESS. God's character, and especially his persevering steadfast love, is continually shown to Jacob. He recognizes that "I am not worthy of the least of all the deeds of steadfast love and all the faithfulness that you have shown to your servant" (Gen. 32:10). God's mercy, not Jacob's merit, is the basis of God's blessing. Even when Jacob waits too long at Shechem and reverts to the old Jacob, God renews his call to him to go to Bethel, and reaffirms his promises to him (35:1, 9–12). God's steadfast love is not fickle or easily offended. It reflects who he *is*.

GOD'S PROTECTION. When God commanded Jacob to return to the land of his fathers, he promised, "I will be with you" (Gen. 31:3). As Jacob goes on his way, the angels of God meet him and he declares, "This is God's camp!" (32:1–2). Jacob recognizes God's gracious protection and provision (33:5, 11). When Jacob is terrified of the Canaanites and Perizzites after the slaughter in the city of Shechem (34:30), God sends forth "a terror from God" upon the cities that surround him as he moves forward in obedience. As Jacob moves forward in God's purposes, he experiences God's powerful protection. God is the ever-present protector of his people.

Personal Implications

Take some time to reflect on the personal implications of Genesis 32:1–35:29 for your life today. Jot down your reflections under the three headings we have considered and on the passage as a whole:

1. Gospel Glimpses

2. Whole-Bible Connections

3. Theological Soundings

4. Genesis 32:1–35:29

As You Finish This Unit . . .

How has the gospel of Jesus Christ reconciled you not only to God but also to your neighbor? Are there outstanding relationships of brokenness that need to be healed? Jesus instructed us, "First be reconciled to your brother, and then come and offer your gift [to God]" (Matt. 5:24). Similarly, the gospel propels us into healed and reconciled relationships with one another—for "by this all people will know that you are my disciples, if you have love for one another" (John 13:35).

Definitions

[1] **Repentance** – A complete change of heart and mind regarding one's overall attitude toward God and one's individual actions. Rebellion is replaced by obedience, and pleasing oneself by pleasing God. True regeneration and conversion is always accompanied by repentance.

WEEK 10:
JOSEPH'S SLAVERY,
GOD'S PROMISES

Genesis 36:1–41:57

The Place of the Passage

While the story of Jacob has shown the establishment of the twelve tribes of Israel,[1] the story of Joseph shows how God preserved Israel outside the Promised Land. It can be seen as a bridge between the stories of the patriarchs and the events of the book of Exodus. In this opening section of the Joseph story, Joseph's immaturity and hardship lead to painful affliction in Egypt. This paves the way, however, for the dramatic reversal and salvation of the entire family of Israel later on.

The Big Picture

The dreamer Joseph is sold into slavery and forgotten in prison, but God providentially preserves him and his family.

▶ Reflection and Discussion

Read through the entire text for this study, Genesis 36:1–41:57. Then interact with the following questions and record your notes on them concerning this section of Genesis. (For further background, see the *ESV Study Bible*, pages 112–123; also available online at esv.org.)

Genesis 36:1 begins, "These are the generations of Esau (that is, Edom)," and 37:2 begins, "These are the generations of Jacob." This is a common refrain throughout Genesis. While we usually think of the story of our life in terms of our own accomplishments, the story of Esau is told in the generations of those who follow him and the story of Jacob is primarily told in the life of Joseph. What implications might this have toward the orientation of our own lives?

Read Genesis 37:1–11. Joseph's dreams will turn out to be prophetic and accurate. Yet what do we learn of Joseph here, early on? Does he display relational wisdom?

In Genesis 37:12–36 we see a series of unexpected circumstances. Though this chapter is marked by unexpected suffering, God's hand of providence continues to guide, as we will see. How does the unexpected strike

Israel:

_____

_____

_____

_____

_____

_____

Joseph:

_____

_____

_____

_____

_____

Reuben:

_____

_____

_____

_____

_____

_____

While the story of Joseph is dominant in the closing sections of Genesis, Judah makes an unexpected entrance on the scene in Genesis 38. In the conspiracy against Joseph, Judah took the initiative to sell Joseph into slavery rather than kill him (37:26–27). Yet in chapter 38, we see that the sin of the Canaanites infiltrates the family of Israel through Judah. What compromises do you see by Judah and his family here?

_____

_____

_____

_____

_____

_____

Against the darkness of Judah's compromise in Genesis 38, Joseph's strong resistance to temptation in chapter 39 shines brightly. How does Joseph deliberately respond to the temptations of Potiphar's wife in this chapter?

Despite God's wonderful plans for Joseph, he goes from slavery to prison. What marks of Joseph's integrity and ongoing trust in God are evident even while he is in prison, as narrated in Genesis 40?

Despite Joseph's integrity in Potiphar's house, he is imprisoned. Despite his integrity and interpretation of dreams in prison, he is forgotten. Yet God forges Joseph's character in the dungeon. Read Genesis 41:1–36. Even after years of being forgotten in prison, Joseph does not show any traces of bitterness. What evidence do you see of Joseph's humble dependence on God to interpret Pharaoh's dream?

As a result, Pharaoh himself recognizes that Joseph has the Spirit of God in him and immediately promotes him to second in his land. Read Genesis 41:37–57. How is God's favor abundantly evident in Joseph's life here?

Read through the following three sections on *Gospel Glimpses, Whole-Bible Connections*, and *Theological Soundings*. Then take time to reflect on the *Personal Implications* these sections may have for your walk with the Lord.

▶ ## Gospel Glimpses

JUDAH. Judah is clearly the black sheep of the family of Israel—intermarrying with the Canaanites, failing to care properly for Tamar his daughter-in-law, and inadvertently sleeping with her and having twins by her. Against the shining story of Joseph's integrity, Judah's compromise appears heinous. However, Judah's failure does not remove him from the activity of God's grace. Later, Jacob blesses him: "The scepter shall not depart from Judah, nor the ruler's staff from between his feet, until tribute comes to him; and to him shall be the obedience of the peoples" (Gen. 49:10). In the ensuing story line of Scripture, the tribe of Judah emerges as the line that would produce King David and ultimately King Jesus. Here again, God's grace rules over and even defies human merit as he uses people in his redemptive purposes.

FROM SLAVES TO KINGS. Joseph makes the unexpected journey from slavery to second in command of the entire nation of Egypt. This journey precipitates Israel's journey from slavery in Egypt to become God's firstborn son (Ex. 4:22) and "a kingdom of priests and a holy nation" (Ex. 19:6). Similarly, Christ rescues us from slavery to sin so that we might be "a chosen race, a royal priesthood, a holy nation, a people for his own possession" (1 Pet. 2:9). Born into spiritual slavery, we are graced with undeserved royal dignity as God's own children, all through the work of Jesus on our behalf.

▶ ## Whole-Bible Connections

AFFLICTION AND FRUITFULNESS. Joseph names his second child Ephraim (which means "fruitfulness"), "For God has made me fruitful in the land of my affliction" (Gen. 41:52). This fulfills God's original command in Genesis 1:28, "Be fruitful and multiply and fill the earth." While the children of Israel do not fill the earth, Joseph's fruitfulness paves the way for the Israelites to fill the land of Egypt (Ex. 1:7). Affliction sets the context for Joseph's fruitfulness (Ex. 1:11–12), just as Genesis 3:16 had predicted. His affliction as a slave of Potiphar and prisoner in Egypt foreshadow the affliction of Israel as slaves of Pharaoh in Egypt. Just as God makes Joseph fruitful in the land of his affliction, so he "has taken [Israel] and brought [Israel] out of the iron furnace, out of Egypt, to be a people of his own inheritance, as you are this day" (Deut. 4:20).

The supreme and ultimate instance in the Bible of God bringing fruitfulness out of affliction is Christ himself, whose affliction at the cross was the means of the most glorious fruit the world has ever known —glory for himself and eternal life for sinners.

SOJOURNING.[2] This is a clear motif for the patriarchs. Genesis 37:1 begins, "Jacob lived in the land of his father's sojournings, in the land of Canaan." At the end of his life, Jacob tells Pharaoh, "The days of the years of my sojourning are 130 years" (Gen. 47:9). Similarly Abraham (Gen. 23:4) views himself as a sojourner in the land. As sojourners, they have settled in the land for some time and have a certain status but are not permanent residents. Israel is repeatedly referred to as a stranger and sojourner before the Lord (Lev. 25:23; 1 Chron. 29:15; Ps. 39:12; 119:19). One consequence is that land is seen as perpetually belonging to the Lord and must not be sold permanently (Lev. 25:23). In the New Testament, Peter picks up this theme in his call for holiness: "Beloved, I urge you as sojourners and exiles to abstain from the passions of the flesh, which wage war against your soul" (1 Pet. 2:11). We are enabled to do this knowing that Christ left his home in heaven to sojourn among us, dying for us, so that we might be fully restored to our true home, God himself (John 6:51).

> ## Theological Soundings

SPIRIT OF GOD. Joseph is clearly seen by Pharaoh to be a man "in whom is the Spirit of God" (Gen. 41:38) because of his ability to interpret dreams. The Spirit (=breath) of God was breathed into all humanity at creation (Gen. 2:7; Job 33:4) and frequently is the means by which supernatural revelation is made through human vessels (Num. 24:2; 2 Sam. 23:2; Neh. 9:30; Isa. 61:1–4; Ezek. 2:2; 11:24; 37:1; Mic. 3:8; Zech. 7:12). Also, the Spirit of God brings an anointing for leadership to Joseph (Gen. 41:38), the seventy elders of Israel (Num. 11:16–29), Joshua (Deut. 34:9), Gideon (Judg. 6:34), Saul (1 Sam. 11:6), and David (1 Sam. 16:13). In the New Testament, the Holy Spirit mediates knowledge of Jesus after he ascends into heaven (John 14:15–26; 16:13–14; Eph. 3:2–6), unites us with Christ to share in his kingdom (Rom. 14:17) and be a part of his body (1 Cor. 12:12–13; Gal. 3:26–29; Eph. 4:13–16), assures believers that they are children and heirs of God (Rom. 8:12–17; Gal. 4:6; 1 John 3:24), gives gifts for ministry (Rom. 12:3–13; 1 Corinthians 12; Eph. 4:7–16), and prays for the believer (Rom. 8:26–27). The Spirit comes down upon the church at Pentecost (Acts 2:1–3) and lives within every believer (Rom. 8:9).

REVELATION. Time and again in the story of Joseph we see that God reveals things through dreams (Gen. 37:5–9; 40:5–19; 41:14–36). Prophecy is later linked with dreams but can be either accurate or misleading (Deut. 13:1–5). Dreams could be valid means of revelation (e.g., 1 Sam. 28:6), or invalid (Jer.

23:25–32). The outpouring of God's Spirit would give revelation through dreams (Joel 2:28; Acts 2:17). In Matthew, five dreams are given in connection with Christ's birth and infancy (Matt. 1:20; 2:12–13, 19, 22). Revelation through dreams is decidedly secondary, however, to the final and clear revelation through the person, teachings, and saving action of the Son, Jesus Christ (Heb. 1:1–3).

▶ **Personal Implications**

Take some time to reflect on the personal implications of Genesis 37:1–41:57 for your life today. Jot down your reflections under the three headings we have considered and on the passage as a whole:

1. Gospel Glimpses

2. Whole-Bible Connections

3. Theological Soundings

4. Genesis 37:1–41:57

As You Finish This Unit . . .

God clearly forms Joseph's character in the dungeon of affliction. How is God forming your character in the dungeon of affliction? How has God used seasons when you felt forgotten or neglected by God to forge your character? How might God be forging your character today? Take some time to recognize God's shaping hand even in the dungeons of affliction today.

Definitions

[1] **Israel** – Originally, a name God gave to Jacob (Gen. 32:28), meaning that he had striven with God. Later applied to the nation formed by his descendants, then to the ten northern tribes of that nation. In the NT, the name is applied to the church as the spiritual descendants of Abraham (Gal. 6:16).

[2] **Sojourner** – One living as a non-citizen in a foreign land. In OT times, sojourners had few rights and were especially vulnerable to mistreatment. The Law of Moses protected sojourners and encouraged the Israelites to include them in community life (see Ex. 22:21; Num. 15:15).

WEEK 11: JOSEPH'S RECONCILIATION

Genesis 42:1–47:31

Stories of reconciliation dominate the book of Genesis. We have already seen the story of Jacob's reconciliation with Esau. In Genesis 42–47 we see Joseph's reconciliation with his brothers and reunion with his father. This story shows the end result of Joseph's experience in the dungeon and the fruit of the ongoing activity of God's grace in Joseph's life. Overall, the journey to Egypt in this section fulfills God's promise to Abraham in Gen. 15:12–16, and sets the stage for the exodus.

The Big Picture

Joseph reconciles with his brothers and brings his family down to Egypt.

Reflection and Discussion

Read through the entire text for this study, Genesis 42:1–47:31. Then interact with the following questions and record your notes on them concerning this section of Genesis. (For further background, see the *ESV Study Bible*, pages 123–132; also available online at esv.org.)

Famine drives the sons of Israel to Egypt again. Just as famine drove Abraham to Egypt (Gen. 12:10) and Isaac toward Egypt (though he sojourns in Gerar instead; Gen. 26:1–4), so famine drives the sons of Israel to Egypt to buy grain. Joseph's dream that his brothers would bow down to him is fulfilled in 42:6. Read through chapters 42–44 and jot down notes on how the pain and scars from the past still affect the following people in Genesis:

Jacob/Israel:

Joseph:

Reuben:

Judah:

Joseph clearly struggles with conflicted emotions toward his brothers through-out chapters 42–44. How do we see this?

Genesis 45 provides the climax to the whole Joseph story (Genesis 37–50). Imagine the feelings of the brothers at Joseph's declaration, "I am Joseph! Is my father still alive?" (45:3). He does not explode in vindictive anger but is gracious and compassionate. Read 45:4–8 carefully. How does Joseph interpret his many years of affliction?

In Genesis 45:16–46:34, we read the moving account of the restoration of Joseph to his father Jacob, who thought that his son was dead. Once Jacob hears the news that Joseph is alive and sees the wagons that Joseph has sent, his spirit revives. The narrator begins to call him Israel consistently from this point forward. What characteristics of Israel, the overcomer, do you see in this section? How is God's blessing seen in his life?

In Genesis 47:1–12, Jacob's family settles in Goshen as shepherds in that land. God had earlier promised Abraham, "in you all the families of the earth shall be blessed" (Gen. 12:3). How does Jacob advance this prophecy as he appears before Pharaoh?

While Adam and Eve were commanded to "Be *fruitful* and *multiply* and fill the earth" (Gen. 1:28), the Israelites "were *fruitful* and *multiplied* greatly" (47:27)—but in Egypt, rather than in the Promised Land of Canaan! In light of God's promise to bless all the families on the earth in Abraham's offspring (12:3), how should we put together Israel's multiplying in Egypt with God's desire to bring blessing to all nations?

Read through the following three sections on *Gospel Glimpses, Whole-Bible Connections*, and *Theological Soundings*. Then take time to reflect on the *Personal Implications* these sections may have for your walk with the Lord.

Gospel Glimpses

TRANSFORMATION. God's work in Jacob's life is ongoing. In Genesis 42:4, Jacob is gripped by fear once again. Like his fear in meeting Esau (Gen. 32:7), he is afraid to send his son Benjamin to buy grain in Egypt (42:4). Only after much convincing does he send Benjamin to Egypt, trusting in God's mercy (43:14). Jacob's fear does not, however, exempt him from God's purposes. God continually pursues Jacob, and God himself assures Jacob about the patriarch's own trip to Egypt: "I am God, the God of your father. Do not be afraid to go down to Egypt, for there I will make you into a great nation" (Gen. 46:3). God's goodness to his children is all out of proportion to what they deserve.

GOD IN EGYPT. God's work is not limited to the land of Canaan; he saves the family of Israel in Egypt through Joseph. Before Stephen's martyrdom in Acts 7, he recounts a summary of gracious salvation history to demonstrate that God's presence was not limited to the temple in Jerusalem. God appeared to Abraham in Mesopotamia (Acts 7:2), to Joseph in Egypt (7:9–10), to Moses in the wilderness (7:30–34), and to Israel at Mount Sinai (7:38). God cannot be limited to any one location, traveling as he did in the "tent of witness in the wilderness" (7:44). Even Solomon's temple[1] could not contain him (7:48–50). This summary of salvation history provides the theological foundation for the gospel to expand outward from Jerusalem into Judea and Samaria (8:1). We must not limit God to any one location, but recognize that he is Lord over all and in all places.

Whole-Bible Connections

EGYPT. In Genesis, Egypt is a haven of protection from famine. Abraham flees to Egypt in the face of famine (Gen. 12:10), and Isaac desired to flee there too

(26:1). Just as Isaac was tempted to trust in Egypt in time of famine (26:1), so Egypt embodies the political and military temptation to trust in another nation instead of the Lord in times of crisis (Isa. 30:1–5; 31:1–7; 36:4–10; Jeremiah 42–43), as Israel commits spiritual adultery with other empires and gods instead of being faithful to the Lord (Ezekiel 23). While Egypt begins as a place of slavery (Gen. 37:36) and imprisonment for Joseph (39:20), it becomes a place of blessing for Joseph (41:52) and the family of Israel (47:27–28). However, with the coming of a new king, Egypt once again becomes a place of slavery (Ex. 1:8–10). Israel's slavery in Egypt becomes the basis for a call to treat aliens differently in Israel (e.g., Ex. 23:9; Lev. 19:34; Deut. 5:12–15). Yet Israel herself becomes oppressive like Egypt and so suffers Egypt's punishment (Amos 3:1–2, 9–10; 8:8). In the New Testament, Jerusalem is figuratively called Egypt because of its murder of Christ and his two witnesses, representing martyred believers (Rev. 11:8).

FAMINE plays a large role in this story of Joseph (Gen. 41:57), just as it did with Abraham (12:10) and Isaac (26:1). In all these contexts, famine provokes migration to a new land, just as it does later for Naomi's husband (Ruth 1:1) and in the days of Elisha (2 Kings. 8:1). Famine is later associated with God's judgment (Deut. 32:24; 2 Sam. 21:1; Ps. 105:16; Isa. 14:30; 51:19; Jer. 11:22; 14:11–18), a curse particularly associated with breaking God's covenant (Deuteronomy 28). In the new earth, the abundance of Eden will be restored (Amos 9:11–15).

Theological Soundings

PROVIDENCE.[2] God's providence does not negate the role of human agency. While the brothers sell Joseph to a caravan (Gen. 37:28; 45:4–5), an action they recognize as sin (42:22; 50:17), Joseph says, "God sent me before you. . . . it was not you who sent me here, but God" (45:7–8). "God meant it for good" (50:20). The good that Joseph recognizes is "to preserve for you a remnant on earth, and to keep alive for you many survivors" (45:7). God's providence does not deny human agency. God is sovereign, *and* humans are responsible. This holds true even for human actions that are sinful. Without in any way sinning himself (James 1:13, 17), God rules providentially over even over evil. This is proven when the Bible speaks of God foreordaining the crucifixion of Christ (Acts 2:22–23; 4:27–28). A rich confidence in divine providence rescues us from our hearts becoming mired in resentment and bitterness.

Personal Implications

Take some time to reflect on the personal implications of Genesis 42:1–47:31 for your life today. Jot down your reflections under the three headings we have considered and on the passage as a whole:

1. Gospel Glimpses

2. Whole-Bible Connections

3. Theological Soundings

4. Genesis 42:1–47:31

▶ As You Finish This Unit . . .

How can a rich understanding of providence rescue your heart from bitterness? Bring your own resentments for past hurts before the Lord, and ask that he would shine a light on his shaping hand of providence in those situations.

Definitions

[1] **Temple** – A place set aside as holy because of God's presence there. Solomon built the first temple of the Lord in Jerusalem, to replace the portable tabernacle.

[2] **Providence** – God's good, wise, and sovereign guidance and control of all things, by which he supplies all our needs and accomplishes his holy will.

WEEK 12: DEATH AND BLESSING

Genesis 48:1–50:26

The Place of the Passage

Genesis begins with God's blessing upon Adam and the command to "Be fruitful and multiply and fill the earth and subdue it" (Gen. 1:28). This blessing is passed on from Adam to Abraham and his descendants, and Jacob refers to how "God Almighty . . . blessed me and said to me, 'Behold I will make you fruitful and multiply you" (Gen. 48:3–4). The blessing of posterity[1] is fulfilled as Israel has been fruitful and multiplied greatly, filling the land of Egypt (47:27). Similarly, in Genesis 49, Jacob/Israel blesses each of his children, preparing the reader for the story of the growth of Israel in the land of Egypt. The blessing of the land,[2] too, is in view, as Jacob's death brings a return to Canaan to bury him there.

The Big Picture

Jacob blesses his sons and dies in the land of Egypt.

Read through the entire text for this study, Genesis 48:1–50:26. Then interact with the following questions and record your notes on them concerning this section of Genesis. (For further background, see the *ESV Study Bible*, pages 132–137; also available online at esv.org.)

If our focus is only on the high drama of Joseph, then Genesis 48–50 seem anticlimactic. Yet these chapters provide a suitable conclusion to the book of Genesis because they trace out how the promises of offspring, land, and blessing to the nations are fulfilled. In 48:1–7, Jacob looks back to how God revealed himself at Luz/Bethel and promised, "Behold, I will make you fruitful and multiply you, and I will make of you a company of peoples and will give this land to your offspring after you for an everlasting possession" (48:4). How is the blessing of to "make you fruitful and multiply you and . . . make of you a company of peoples" passed on from Jacob to Ephraim and Manasseh in 48:8–22?

How is the blessing of land passed on to Joseph and his sons in Genesis 48:21–22?

While the older is usually blessed before the younger, how does Israel deliberately reverse this? Why do you suppose he does this?

In Genesis 49, Jacob gathers his sons and speaks prophetically over them of "what shall happen to you in days to come" (49:1). Simeon and Levi notably destroyed the city of Shechem after the rape of Dinah. What consequences do they receive?

Although Judah similarly is shown in an unfavorable light in Genesis 38 with the affair with Tamar, Jacob issues an unexpected blessing upon Judah. How is the call to Adam in 1:28 developed in the blessing on Judah in 49:8–12?

How does the blessing given to Joseph in Genesis 49:22–26 develop the call of 1:28?

With the death of Jacob, the focus shifts from the blessing of offspring to the blessing of land. Amid the extensive mourning for Jacob, where is the primary focus for his burial in Genesis 49:28–50:14?

Joseph's brothers panic at the death of their father, fearing that Joseph will lash out against them in revenge. How does an understanding of God's providence help Joseph to deal with his brothers in Genesis 50:15–21?

How are the promises of land and offspring fulfilled through Joseph in Genesis 50:22–26? How does this foreshadow what is to come?

Read through the following three sections on *Gospel Glimpses, Whole-Bible Connections,* and *Theological Soundings*. Then take time to reflect on the *Personal Implications* these sections may have for your walk with the Lord.

▶ Gospel Glimpses

OBEDIENCE OF THE NATIONS. To Judah, Jacob prophesies, "The scepter shall not depart from Judah, nor the ruler's staff from between his feet, until tribute comes to him; and to him shall be the obedience of the peoples" (Gen. 49:10). This prophecy begins to be fulfilled through King David, of the tribe of Judah, but it ultimately is fulfilled in King Jesus. Through Jesus "we have received grace and apostleship to bring about the *obedience* of faith for the sake of his name among all the *nations*" (Rom. 1:5). Similarly, Paul's ministry seeks "what Christ has accomplished . . . to bring the Gentiles to obedience—by word and deed" (Rom. 15:18; cf. 16:26). The obedience of the nations comes through the scepter of King Jesus. This king, however, rules by the saving power of the gospel and not the killing power of the sword.

YOUNGER AND OLDER. Although Jacob was younger, he received the blessing of the older son, and he similarly blesses Joseph's younger son (Ephraim) over the older son (Manasseh). He says about Manasseh, "his younger brother shall be greater than he, and his offspring shall become a multitude of nations"

(Gen. 48:19). Similarly, "God chose what is weak in the world to shame the strong; God chose what is low and despised in the world, even things that are not, to bring to nothing things that are, so that no human being might boast in the presence of God" (1 Cor. 1:27–29). Such radical reversal is present even from the time of the fathers in Genesis. The firstborn frequently do not receive the blessing of God, from Cain (Genesis 4) to Esau (Gen. 25:23) and Reuben (49:3). This gives great hope to us today. God delights to use and enrich those whom the world deems most insignificant.

Whole-Bible Connections

LATTER DAYS. Jacob speaks of what will "happen to you in days to come," which can also be translated "in the latter days" (Gen. 49:1). This expression may be simply a reference to the future, but it may have a more specifically eschatological nuance. It occurs next when Balaam speaks of "what this people will do to your people in the latter days" (Num. 24:14), when "a star shall come out of Jacob, and a scepter shall rise out of Israel [to] crush the forehead of Moab" (Num. 24:17). Jesus himself is "the bright morning star" (Rev. 22:16; cf. 2 Pet. 1:19), who crushes his enemies (Matt. 21:44). Jesus is the cornerstone who falls on his enemies, just as "in the latter days" a stone made without hands would crush the nations that rise up against God (Dan. 2:28, 44–45).

RETURN FROM EGYPT. Egypt is clearly not the final destination for the sons of Israel. Much earlier, God had spoken to Abraham that they would be "sojourners in a land that is not theirs and will be servants there, and they will be afflicted for four hundred years. . . . And they shall come back here in the fourth generation" (Gen. 15:13, 16). Similarly, when Jacob prepares to go down to Egypt to see Joseph, God promises, "I myself will go down with you to Egypt, and I will also bring you up again" (Gen. 46:4). At his own death, Joseph tells his brothers, "I am about to die, but God will visit you and bring you up out of this land to the land that he swore to Abraham, to Isaac, and to Jacob" (Gen. 50:24). Hebrews 11:22 says, "By faith Joseph, at the end of his life, made mention of the exodus of the Israelites and gave directions concerning his bones." This return from Egypt parallels Israel's return from exile that would happen much later, but ultimately it is fulfilled in Jesus' own return from Egypt (Matt. 2:13–15, 19–23).

Theological Soundings

ESCHATOLOGY. "Eschatology" means "the doctrine of last things." Genesis 49:1 addresses what will happen "in the latter days." While this statement may simply mean "in days to come," its later uses suggest a more eschatologically charged sense. While dominion and fruitful procreation were God's original intention in creation (Gen. 1:28), we see that Jacob looks forward to dominion especially through Judah (Gen. 49:8–12) and fruitful procreation especially through Joseph (Gen. 49:22–26). Jacob sees that God's purposes at the beginning of creation are fulfilled at the end. Eschatology (what happens at the end) reflects and fulfills protology (what happened at the beginning).

GOD'S FAITHFULNESS. As Jacob nears the end of his life, God's abundant faithfulness gives him confidence that his children will become a multitude (Gen. 48:16) and will return to the land of their fathers (v. 21). He is "the God before whom my fathers Abraham and Isaac walked, the God who has been my shepherd all my life long to this day" (v. 15). Similarly, the God of Abraham, Isaac, and Jacob continues to be faithful to his promises, "for all the promises of God find their Yes in [Christ]. That is why it is through him that we utter our Amen to God for his glory" (2 Cor. 1:20). The supreme promise to which God proves faithful is that he will restore his people to himself one day. In Christ, this promise is decisively guaranteed.

> **Personal Implications**

Take some time to reflect on the personal implications of Genesis 48:1–50:26 for your life today. Jot down your reflections under the three headings we have considered and on the passage as a whole:

1. Gospel Glimpses

2. Whole-Bible Connections

3. Theological Soundings

4. Genesis 48:1–50:26

▶ As You Finish This Unit . . .

Genesis ends with a microcosmic fulfillment of God's purposes, as Israel settles in the land of Egypt, is fruitful, and multiplies greatly. This microcosmic picture points forward to a more macrocosmic fulfillment that is ultimately fulfilled in Christ. Think about the world in which we live. How are the promises to Abraham being fulfilled in the advance of the gospel throughout the world today? Take time to praise God and pray that these purposes would be completely fulfilled.

▶ As You Finish Studying Genesis . . .

We rejoice with you as you finish studying the book of Genesis! May this study become part of your Christian walk of faith, day-by-day and week-by-week throughout all your life. Now we would greatly encourage you to study the Word of God on a week-by-week basis. To continue your study of the Bible, we would encourage you to consider other books in the Knowing the Bible series, and to visit www.knowingthebibleseries.org.

Lastly, take a moment to look back through this study. Review the notes that you have written, and the things that you have highlighted or underlined. Reflect again on the key themes that the Lord has been teaching you about himself and about his Word. May these things become a treasure for you throughout your life—which we pray will be true for you, in the name of the Father, and the Son, and the Holy Spirit. Amen.

Definitions

[1] **Posterity** – The line of offspring and children. This is of particular importance in Genesis because of the prominence of genealogies tracing the offspring of Eve who will crush the head of the offspring of the serpent (Gen. 3:15).

[2] **Land** – Beginning in Gen. 12:1–3, God repeatedly promises Abraham and his offspring the Promised Land, where they would live.

KNOWING THE BIBLE STUDY GUIDE SERIES

Experience the *Grace* of God in the *Word* of God, Book by Book

— Series Volumes —

- Genesis
- Exodus
- Leviticus
- Numbers
- Deuteronomy
- Joshua
- Judges
- Ruth and Esther
- 1–2 Samuel
- 1–2 Kings
- 1–2 Chronicles
- Ezra and Nehemiah
- Job
- Psalms
- Proverbs
- Ecclesiastes
- Song of Solomon

- Isaiah
- Jeremiah
- Lamentations, Habakkuk, and Zephaniah
- Ezekiel
- Daniel
- Hosea
- Joel, Amos, and Obadiah
- Jonah, Micah, and Nahum
- Haggai, Zechariah, and Malachi
- Matthew
- Mark
- Luke

- John
- Acts
- Romans
- 1 Corinthians
- 2 Corinthians
- Galatians
- Ephesians
- Philippians
- Colossians and Philemon
- 1–2 Thessalonians
- 1–2 Timothy and Titus
- Hebrews
- James
- 1–2 Peter and Jude
- 1–3 John
- Revelation

crossway.org/knowingthebible